Millennium in the Middle

Millennium in the Middle

*Reconciling Dispensational Longing
with Amillennial Hope*

KEVIN GOODMAN

WIPF & STOCK · Eugene, Oregon

MILLENNIUM IN THE MIDDLE
Reconciling Dispensational Longing with Amillennial Hope

Copyright © 2025 Kevin Goodman. All rights reserved. Except for brief quotations in critical publications or reviews, no part of this book may be reproduced in any manner without prior written permission from the publisher. Write: Permissions, Wipf and Stock Publishers, 199 W. 8th Ave., Suite 3, Eugene, OR 97401.

Wipf & Stock
An Imprint of Wipf and Stock Publishers
199 W. 8th Ave., Suite 3
Eugene, OR 97401

www.wipfandstock.com

PAPERBACK ISBN: 979-8-3852-6482-7
HARDCOVER ISBN: 979-8-3852-6483-4
EBOOK ISBN: 979-8-3852-6484-1

VERSION NUMBER 122225

Scripture quotations are from the ESV® Bible (The Holy Bible, English Standard Version®), © 2001 by Crossway, a publishing ministry of Good News Publishers. Used by permission. All rights reserved.

This book is dedicated to my beautiful wife, Kharissa, who set me on this journey. Thank you for always asking the hard questions, forcing me into deeper personal study.

Contents

Preface | ix

Chapter 1
What Exactly Is the Millennium? | 1

Chapter 2
The Roots of Amillennialism | 23

Chapter 3
Satan Bound? A Closer Look at Revelation 20 | 41

Chapter 4
What Comes Next? | 62

Chapter 5
Israel and the End of Days: God's Plan, Our Posture | 83

Chapter 6
Objections to the Hybrid Approach | 98

Chapter 7
A Pastoral Approach to Eschatology | 120

Appendix
Exegesis of Key Texts from the Dispensational Amillennial Perspective | 143

Bibliography | 153

Preface

IN THE TWENTIETH CENTURY, the world faced a looming crisis: population was growing faster than food production. Famines threatened entire regions. Scientists and farmers knew that if nothing changed, millions could starve.

Then came Norman Borlaug, a plant scientist who did not try to reinvent the wheel—he just asked a better question: "What if we took the strongest qualities from multiple wheat strains and combined them?"[1]

What followed was the development of hybrid wheat—a crossbreed that was high-yielding, disease-resistant, and adaptable to harsh climates. It did not belong to any one strain or tradition. It was the best of several lines, integrated with purpose.

The result? A global agricultural transformation. This one idea—strategic hybridization—is credited with saving over a billion lives.

This book is driven by a similar question.

In the world of eschatology, we often inherit theological "strains" that are strong in some areas but weak in others. Some emphasize a literal reading of prophetic Scripture, rooted in God's promises to Israel. Others focus on the present reign of Christ, the simplicity of the gospel, and the church's mission now.

What if we did not have to choose between them?

---

1. Borlaug, "Nobel Prize Lecture."

Preface

What if amillennialism, often misunderstood and under-explored, holds a key not to replace but to strengthen the system many of us grew up with?

That is my aim here: not to tear down what has come before but to offer a hybrid perspective—one that honors the covenant promises of God, recognizes the literary form of apocalyptic texts, and centers everything on the finished work of Christ.

I am not asking you to abandon your framework. I am asking you to reconsider how all the pieces might fit together if we allowed the Bible, not a chart, to lead the conversation.

Like Borlaug's wheat, the result may surprise you—not by how radically different it looks, but by how much more fruitful it becomes.

I grew up in a traditional Southern Baptist church for all my life. When the pastor(s) approached matters of eschatology, I heard one view and one view only. It is likely the view you have heard as well: we live in the church age and next on the calendar is the rapture of the church, followed by the great tribulation. Oddly, of all the pastors I ever heard speak, I never heard one mention that there were other views. I also noticed that every pastor seemed to avoid any mention of the millennium mentioned in Rev 20. Possibly because this idea confuses many, and possibly because it's only mentioned in one passage in the whole entire Bible.

I was serving as a pastor of a church when my wife was attending a women's Bible study on the book of Revelation and she asked me a series questions about the millennium. I had a canned answer in my head, but the questions she posed, about death and deception after Christ returned, threw me for a loop, caused me to study for myself, and come up with my own conclusion(s).

The more I thought about it, I found that much of what I believe was not because I came to that belief but rather because I had been taught it by someone else. I asked myself the question, would I believe this if I had not been taught this? I was surprised to learn how many in my own denomination hold a different view, and how the Baptist faith and message leaves matters of eschatology open to the believer.

Preface

After much study, I have come to a different conclusion than most, and I would have to call myself a "dispensational amillennialist." I consider this to be like the wheat: a hybrid version of dispensationalism and amillennialism, meaning that I hold traditional views of dispensationalism, excluding a literal thousand-year reign of Christ on earth. I very much believe in a seven-year tribulation, I believe in an antichrist, and I am open to belief in a pre-tribulation rapture.

But I believe when Christ comes, Satan is defeated once and for all. It is a very nuanced view and I have not met anyone that believes quite like me on the matter, and I am humble enough to admit I could be wrong. Because my views are unique and somewhat complex, this book is an attempt to clarify my personal views on the matter.

When it comes to eschatology—the study of the end times—there is one truth nearly everyone agrees on: none of us has it all figured out. Jesus himself told his disciples that certain details of his return and the unfolding of future events were not for them to know (Acts 1:7). If the original apostles did not get a full timeline, perhaps we should approach this subject with a dose of humility.

This book is written not as a theological hammer but as an invitation—an invitation to consider a different way of looking at the millennium mentioned in Rev 20. For many readers, the term "amillennialism" may sound strange, maybe even wrong. But I would ask you to hold off judgment, not because I am claiming to be right but because I believe this view deserves a fair and fresh hearing—especially when viewed in a light that is often overlooked: through a dispensational lens.

Now, I realize that may sound contradictory. Dispensationalism and amillennialism are typically seen as theological oil and water. One emphasizes a future reign of Christ on earth, a restored Israel, and a literal thousand years. The other often emphasizes the present reign of Christ, a fulfilled kingdom, and a symbolic interpretation of Rev 20. But what if there is more overlap than we have admitted? What if these views are not as incompatible as they seem?

Preface

Let me be clear: I could be wrong. Eschatology is a complex and mysterious subject. Every view—whether it is premillennialism, postmillennialism, amillennialism, historic premillennialism, or even "pan millennialism" ("It'll all pan out in the end")—has its strengths and its challenges. Some emphasize the hope of Christ's return but struggle with the sequence of resurrections. Others offer a powerful now-and-not-yet theology but have difficulty with Israel's future. And some rely so heavily on literalism or symbolism that they risk missing the heart of the message: Jesus wins.

This book is not about tearing down anyone else's view. It is about opening a door that may have been closed too quickly. If you are curious about the end times, if you have struggled to make sense of Revelation, or if you have never heard an amillennial perspective explained in a way that appreciates dispensational distinctives, then this book is for you.

You do not have to agree with every page. I do not even expect you to. But I do hope you will finish this book with a deeper appreciation for the complexity of God's plan, a greater longing for Christ's return, and a willingness to say, like I do: "I might not have every detail right, but I want to be faithful in how I think, live, and teach about his coming kingdom."

Let's begin—with open Bibles, open hearts, and open minds.

Chapter 1

What Exactly Is the Millennium?

FEW TOPICS IN CHRISTIAN theology ignite more debate—or more confusion—than the "millennium." The word "millennium" doesn't appear in Scripture at all—yet Revelation 20's description of "a thousand years" has produced entire systems of eschatology, denominational divides, conferences, charts, and late-night YouTube rabbit holes.

So, what exactly is the millennium?

The word comes from the Latin phrase *mille annus*, meaning a thousand years. Revelation 20:1–6 describes a period in which Satan is bound, Christ reigns, and certain believers come to life and rule with him. It sounds glorious—and mysterious. But is it literal? Future? Spiritual? Present?

How you answer that depends largely on which theological tradition you come from—and which assumptions you're willing to challenge.

Let us look at the text. Here is what Rev 20:1–6 actually says:

> Then I saw an angel coming down from heaven, holding in his hand the key to the bottomless pit and a great chain. And he seized the dragon, that ancient serpent, who is the devil and Satan, and bound him for a thousand years . . . so that he might not deceive the nations

any longer. . . . They came to life and reigned with Christ for a thousand years. (ESV)

This is the *only* passage in the Bible that mentions a thousand-year reign of Christ explicitly.

Below are the three major views at a glance, defined:

- Premillennialism: Christ returns before the thousand years and reigns on earth during that time.
- Postmillennialism: Christ returns after the thousand years—a golden age of gospel growth and global peace.
- Amillennialism: The thousand years is symbolic, referring to the current church age where Christ reigns spiritually from heaven.

Each view has its merits, and each has its questions to answer.

What makes the millennium so difficult to interpret? There are three primary reasons to consider:

1. **It is Apocalyptic Literature.** Revelation is filled with symbolism—beasts, horns, dragons, lampstands, and seals. So, is the "thousand years" symbolic, too?
2. **It is Isolated.** No other passage in Scripture mentions a literal thousand-year reign of Christ. That does not mean it is not real—but it does mean we have to handle it carefully.
3. **It is Not Chronologically Clear.** Revelation is not necessarily written in strict chronological order. Does Rev 20 follow Rev 19 in time? Or is it a new vision?

Why does it matter?

Because what we believe about the millennium affects how we view

- Christ's current reign
- Satan's power
- the church's role
- our hope

What Exactly Is the Millennium?

To begin, I would like you, the reader, to carefully consider the weakness of each of the major views. Anyone that says their view does not have a weakness either has not studied it in detail or is outright lying. If one is going to preach or teach effectively, they must have a dose of humility—that begins by being honest with weaknesses. Let us begin with the most popular of the three, premillennialism.

Weaknesses of Premillennialism

Premillennialism has been the dominant eschatological view in much of modern evangelicalism, especially within dispensational circles. **Dispensationalism** is a theological system that views God's plan for history as unfolding in a series of distinct periods, or *dispensations*, in which he relates to humanity in different ways. It emphasizes a literal interpretation of Scripture, a clear distinction between Israel and the church, and the belief that God will fulfill his promises to Israel in a future earthly kingdom under the reign of Christ.

While it is built on a high view of Scripture and a desire to take prophecy seriously, it also presents several significant theological and interpretive challenges—particularly surrounding the concept of a litera thousand-year earthly reign of Christ. Let's explore some of those.

First, we should consider the isolation of Rev 20; comparing Daniel and Revelation, there are correlating verses to support seven-year tribulation, an antichrist, and Jesus even referenced what many believe to be the abomination of desolation in a third temple. However, when it comes to this thousand-year reign, there is one passage and one passage alone.

Problem: The entire doctrine of a future thousand-year reign rests on one passage alone—Rev 20:1–6.

Weakness: No other book in the Bible clearly mentions this millennium. If it were such a central doctrine, why is it never referenced in the teachings of Jesus, the epistles, or Old Testament prophecy in explicit terms?

Implication: Building a full timeline around an apocalyptic vision—known for symbolism—runs the risk of over-literalizing what may be metaphorical.

Secondly, there is the hugely problematic post-glory rebellion. This is the problem that set me on my journey. I just have not been able to reconcile a future post-glory rebellion. In the Bible, I consistently read of a future hope and future kingdom where there will be no more pain, no more suffering. I do not read of a future kingdom that will include pain, suffering, rebellion, even death—only to be followed by another kingdom. Some have attempted to answer this, but I have not found a satisfactory answer yet. A post-glory rebellion while Jesus is physically reigning is hard for anyone to clearly defend.

Problem: In premillennialism, Christ returns in glory, reigns on earth with resurrected saints, and yet, somehow, Satan is released and leads a massive global rebellion (Rev 20:7–9).

Weakness: How is it plausible that after one thousand years of perfect governance by Christ himself—visible and ruling from Jerusalem—the nations would be so easily deceived again?

Theological tension: Why would God allow rebellion after he has already conquered and judged? What purpose does it serve?

Third, there is the multifaceted problem of two resurrections, two judgments, and two classes of people. This problem really speaks for itself when you consider it. Imagine having your neighbor, who has already died, come back to life in a glorified body, yet you are awaiting death after Christ has returned and sits on a literal throne in the world in which you live. If you were to get sick, would you even seek treatment? This is a hard reality for me to imagine. I suppose it is not impossible, but it is hard to comprehend and hard to explain.

Problem: Premillennialism requires a complicated structure—one resurrection for the righteous at Christ's return, another resurrection for the wicked one thousand years later, and saints with glorified bodies coexisting with mortal unbelievers

Weakness: This scenario creates major theological and practical difficulties. What does evangelism or sin look like when glorified saints live next door? Why are mortals judged twice—once by living under Christ, and again at the final judgment?

The fourth problem is the problem of postponement theology.

Problem: Dispensational premillennialism teaches that Christ offered the kingdom during his first coming, but it was rejected by Israel and postponed until after the rapture and tribulation.

Weakness: This creates a "Plan B" view of history and undermines the idea that Christ's life, death, and resurrection were the full unfolding of God's redemptive plan.

Contrast: Jesus did not say the kingdom would come later—he said, "The kingdom of God is at hand" (Mark 1:15).

Fifth is the glaring silence on the millennium in Paul's theology. The apostle Paul wrote much about eschatology. He references several things that could be interpreted different ways, yet when it comes to a thousand-year reign of Christ, he is oddly silent. This event, if it were literal, would be something to write about, and even warn others about, yet he did not do so.

Problem: The apostle Paul wrote extensively about resurrection, the return of Christ, and judgment—but never mentions a literal thousand-year reign.

Weakness: If Paul taught about rapture, resurrection, and final judgment occurring together (1 Cor 15; 1 Thess 4–5), how do we insert a thousand-year gap between them?

It is a safe conclusion that Paul presents a single return, a single resurrection, and a single final judgement—not a split-stage return of Christ.

Sixth, this eschatology belief has Old Testament prophecies read without New Testament fulfillment.

Problem: A common misuse of Old Testament prophecy in discussions of the millennium arises when passages like Isa 65:17–25 are read through a strictly dispensational or premillennial lens. Many interpreters claim this text depicts the conditions of the millennial kingdom—a restored Israel enjoying peace, longevity, and prosperity under Christ's earthly reign. However, a careful reading of the text itself shows that the prophecy moves beyond the temporal restoration of Israel and speaks of a reality that follows the ultimate renewal of creation: "For behold, I create new heavens and a new earth, and the former things shall not be remembered or come into mind" (Isa 65:17 ESV). The language of newness, unbroken joy, and absence of former sorrows clearly places this passage after the final judgment and the inauguration of the new heavens and new earth, not during a transitional earthly kingdom.

Misapplying this prophecy and others to the millennium distorts its original intent and conflates God's final eschatological renewal with an interim kingdom period. Isaiah 65 is not a blueprint for a thousand-year reign but a vision of *God's ultimate restoration*, when sin, death, and sorrow are finally abolished. Using it to predict temporal earthly conditions in the millennium overlooks the text's temporal markers and theological context, which emphasize the *completion of God's redemptive plan* rather than a provisional kingdom for Israel alone. The passage, therefore, belongs in *eschatological fulfillment after Christ's return, judgment, and the consummation of all things*, pointing to the eternal state rather than an intermediate kingdom.

This view teaches, based on some Old Testament prophecies, that temple worship, feasts, and even sacrifices will occur in this literal thousand-year reign. Classic premillennial dispensationalism unintentionally reopens what God has forever closed. They would say it would not be the remission of sins but rather, as a memorial, much like the Lord's Supper we celebrate today. But by reintroducing sacrifices and feasts after the cross, it places shadows back where the substance has already come.

The veil was torn for a reason—Christ has fulfilled every offering, every feast, and every symbol. The temple stood as a promise; Calvary made it a memory. To reinstate sacrifices in a future millennium is to hang the veil back up and act as though redemption was unfinished. But as Jesus declared at the cross, "It is finished."

Weakness: They often ignore how the New Testament authors reinterpret those promises considering Christ (see Acts 2, Gal 3, Heb 8–10). The Bible is quite clear—Jesus will not become the high priest; he has already become the high priest.

What Exactly Is the Millennium?

Alternative: Amillennialism says the promises are fulfilled—in Christ, in the church, and ultimately, in the new creation.

The seventh and last problem I will mention is the nature of the kingdom itself.

Problem: Premillennialism insists on a geopolitical, national, and physical kingdom of Christ centered in Jerusalem.

Weakness: Jesus said his kingdom "is not of this world" (John 18:36), and Paul said it is "not a matter of eating and drinking, but of righteousness, peace, and joy in the Holy Spirit" (Rom 14:17).

Implication: A focus on an earthly throne may distract from the spiritual reign of Christ already underway.

Premillennialism Conclusion: Complication Without Clarity

While premillennialism seeks to take prophecy seriously, it introduces layers of complexity—multiple comings, judgments, resurrections, rebellions—that often conflict with the simpler, unified eschatology presented in the rest of the New Testament.

That does not mean premillennialists are insincere or unfaithful—it means we must ask whether the system aligns with the Bible's broader redemptive story or whether it overlays a timeline onto a text that was never meant to function that way.

It does not even mean that premillennialists are wrong; it just means there are unexplained holes in their eschatology. But as you will see, the other views have unexplained weaknesses as well.

Now let us consider **postmillennialism**. If there were a correct view, I would like to adhere to it would be this one. I would love to know that the world in which I live would continue to get better, the gospel would advance, and there are only good times ahead. But this seems to go against what the Bible teaches, and it seems to be counterintuitive to history. Let us consider the weakness of this view.

Weaknesses of Postmillennialism—Optimism with Some Oversight

Postmillennialism offers a compelling vision: the gospel will so powerfully influence the world that, over time, the nations will be discipled, peace will reign, and Christ will return after this "golden age" of gospel success. It emphasizes hope, cultural engagement, and the ongoing triumph of the church in history.

At first glance, it seems attractive—especially as a counter to defeatism in the church. But this view, too, has several significant weaknesses—both scriptural and historical—that cannot be ignored.

First, this view is overly optimistic about human progress.

Problem: Postmillennialism envisions a time in history—before Christ's return—when righteousness, justice, and peace dominate global society through the success of the gospel.

Weakness: Scripture and experience suggest otherwise. Jesus described the end as being marked by lawlessness, persecution, and deception (Matt 24:9-12). Paul said things would go "from bad to worse" (2 Tim 3:13), not good to better.

Reality check: The world is not gradually improving in morality. In fact, many regions show increased hostility to Christianity.

Secondly, this view tends to minimize the "already/not yet" tension.

Problem: Postmillennialism can blur the line between the inauguration and the consummation of the kingdom.

Weakness: While the kingdom has come in Christ (Mark 1:15), its full expression—where sin, death, and Satan are completely vanquished—awaits his return (Rev 21:4).

Risk: This view can project too much of the future glory into the present age and ignore the "groaning" that Paul says still defines the world (Rom 8:22-23).

Third, this view places too much confidence in cultural victory. Confidence is a wonderful thing, and "all authority" has indeed been giving to Christ, but that does not mean we are exempt from a rebellion and a great falling away echoed through Scripture. It simply means the gospel will advance.

Problem: Postmillennialism often assumes the church will gain increasing influence over governments, systems, and societies.

Weakness: While cultural influence is not bad, it is not the same as spiritual victory. Nowhere in the New Testament are Christians told they will take over the world before Christ returns.

Biblical emphasis: The church is often described as a suffering, persevering minority (Matt 5:10–12; 1 Pet 4:12–16), not a triumphant majority.

Fourth, this view ignores or downplays global apostasy before the end,

Problem: Postmillennialism expects a global Christianization of culture before the second coming.

Weakness: This is difficult to reconcile with passages like 2 Thess 2, which speaks of a great rebellion (apostasy) and the rise of the "man of lawlessness"; and Matt 24, where Jesus predicts persecution, deception, and tribulation; and the entire book of Revelation, which portrays conflict and suffering right up until the return of Christ.

Implication: A "golden age" of peace and Christian dominance is hard to find in the texts most associated with the end times.

Fifth, this view is subject to historical setbacks.

Problem: Postmillennialism has historically thrived during times of prosperity (e.g., the Enlightenment or the pre-WWI era), when people believed humanity was evolving morally and socially.

Weakness: Major global events like the World Wars, the Holocaust, persecution in China, and moral decline in the West have all but shattered the confidence that society is progressing toward a Christianized utopia.

Observation: Many postmillennial hopes have faded, not because of bad theology but because history itself has been a harsh refutation.

Sixth, at least from my perspective, there is a misuse of Old Testament prophecy.

Problem: Postmillennialism often sees prophecies about peace, prosperity, and worldwide worship (e.g., Isa 2, Ps 72, Mic 4) as being fulfilled before Christ returns.

Weakness: These passages are more accurately understood as describing the new heavens and new earth, not the prereturn world.

Contrast: Amillennialism sees these as fulfilled in part now (in the church age) and fully in the eternal state.

Lastly, this view runs the risk of theological elitism.

Problem: Postmillennialism can foster a superiority mindset—especially among certain reconstructionist or theonomic groups who believe they are building the perfect Christian society.

Weakness: This can lead to division, pride, or an emphasis on dominion over service, power over humility.

Gospel contrast: The message of the cross is one of self-sacrifice and endurance, not dominionism.

Conclusion: Hopeful, but Likely Misplaced

Postmillennialism appeals to our desire for victory, cultural transformation, and global revival. But it puts that hope on the wrong side of Christ's return. It assumes a level of success in the church's mission that neither Scripture nor history promises.

That does not mean postmillennialists are foolish or faithless—they are often passionate, engaged, and mission-minded. But their vision of the future may downplay the suffering, perseverance, and tension that Scripture says will accompany the church until the very end.

In contrast, amillennialism does not say the kingdom will not win. It simply says it is already winning—through weakness, through witness, and through the Spirit—even while we wait for the final victory at Christ's return.

Like I stated earlier, I would love this viewpoint to be true; I just do not see it supported in Scripture. Furthermore, unlike amillennialism, this view seems to stand largely alone. It cannot easily coincide with the other views.

What Exactly Is the Millennium?

Postmillennialism contrasts with both premillennialism and amillennialism in its view of the end times by teaching that the world will gradually improve through the spread of the gospel, leading to a golden age of righteousness before Christ returns. While premillennialism expects worsening conditions and a future earthly reign of Christ after his return, and amillennialism sees the current age as the symbolic millennium marked by both gospel growth and ongoing tribulation, postmillennialism uniquely holds to an optimistic view of history, expecting widespread Christian influence in society prior to the second coming.

So far, you should be able to see clearly the weakness of premillennialism and postmillennialism, but to be fair, we should also consider the weakness of my view, amillennialism.

Weaknesses of Amillennialism—Where Tension Remains

Amillennialism offers a compelling alternative to both premillennialism and postmillennialism. It affirms Christ's present reign, the already/not-yet nature of his kingdom, and a single, climactic return of Christ to judge and renew all things. But like any interpretive framework, amillennialism is not without its tensions.

While I personally hold to this view (as you have read), I also recognize that there are areas where amillennialism faces difficult questions and interpretive challenges. Let us examine those honestly.

The first and major problem is the binding of Satan. Satan bound—really?

Problem: Revelation 20 says Satan is "bound . . . so that he might not deceive the nations" (v. 3), and amillennialism interprets this as a present reality.

Weakness: Many believers struggle to reconcile this with the ongoing reality of evil, deception, persecution, and spiritual darkness.

Tension: If Satan is truly bound, how do we explain false religions, global conflict, and growing hostility to the gospel in many parts of the world?

Clarification Needed: The amillennial answer (that Satan is bound in a limited sense—from preventing global deception, not local temptation) is biblical but requires nuance—and it is not immediately intuitive to all readers.

Secondly, the problem of a symbolic millennium can be seen as too abstract.

Problem: Amillennialism interprets the "one thousand years" symbolically as the "Church Age"—from Christ's resurrection to his return.

Weakness: Some see this as too vague. A symbolic number with no defined beginning or end can feel theologically unsatisfying or too convenient.

Critique: It may appear that amillennialism simply spiritualizes difficult passages rather than dealing with them head-on.

Perception Risk: Critics may assume it downplays prophecy or lacks a clear eschatological timeline (even if that's not true).

The third problem is with the "first resurrection"—is it physical or spiritual?

Problem: Revelation 20:5 speaks of those who partake in the "first resurrection," who reign with Christ for a thousand years.

Amillennial View: This refers to either the believer's spiritual rebirth or their entrance into heaven after physical death.

Weakness: This interpretation feels strained to some, especially when "resurrection" elsewhere consistently means bodily resurrection.

Tension: Is it exegetically consistent to define "resurrection" symbolically in one verse and literally in the next?

The fourth problem many have with this view is Israel's role—is it fulfilled or forgotten?

Problem: Amillennialism teaches that God's promises to Israel are fulfilled in Christ and extended to all believers (Jew and gentile alike).

Weakness: Some readers struggle with this and feel it minimizes the national and ethnic elements of Old Testament prophecy.

Accusation: It's often accused of promoting "replacement theology," even though most amillennialists (myself included) would call it "fulfillment theology."

Challenge: Explaining how Israel's identity fits into the church without erasing it takes careful theological work—and not everyone agrees.

The fifth problem that I have tried to reconcile is underdeveloped views of the tribulation and antichrist.

Problem: Because amillennialism does not require a future seven-year tribulation, it often leaves believers with uncertainty about what to expect before Christ returns.

Weakness: Terms like "antichrist," "man of lawlessness," and "great tribulation" are often interpreted broadly (symbolic of all persecution)—but some readers want clearer answers.

Risk: It can feel like amillennialism is avoiding specifics—especially compared to the detailed charts and sequences in premillennialism.

Sixth, this view is not chart-friendly.

Problem: Amillennialism doesn't lend itself to tidy charts, graphs, or prophecy timelines.

Weakness: For people raised on dispensational prophecy conferences, that can feel frustrating or confusing.

Pastoral Reality: People often want to know what's coming next. Amillennialism's embrace of mystery can be seen as vague or unhelpful in moments of fear or doubt.

Lastly, this view sometimes overcorrects.

Problem: In trying to avoid the literalism of dispensationalism and the optimism of postmillennialism, some amillennial writers swing too far in the other direction.

Weakness: This can lead to an almost fatalistic or overly symbolic reading of prophecy, where everything is spiritualized and nothing is concrete.

Danger: If we are not careful, we can reduce real future hope into metaphor—and lose the comfort of a bodily, visible return of Christ.

Why These Weaknesses Do Not Dismiss the View

Every theological system has tensions. No eschatological model answers every question perfectly. The goal is not to find a view with no weaknesses but to find the one that best aligns with the whole counsel of Scripture.

Amillennialism Still Offers a Deeply Christ-Centered, Gospel-Driven Framework

It affirms a present reign of Christ. It sees suffering and tribulation as part of God's plan—not interruptions. It holds to one final return, one resurrection, and one judgment—a beautifully simple culmination. And it preserves the tension of the "already/not yet"—just like the rest of New Testament theology.

Yes, we must be humble. We must acknowledge that even our best theology is seen through a glass dimly (1 Cor 13:12). But humility does not mean uncertainty. It means standing firm in the truths we can see—while trusting God with what we don't yet understand.

These questions will be taken up more fully in the chapters ahead, but for now, let's step back and consider how we should approach eschatology as Christians. I will even explain how amillennialism can be viewed in a new light worth considering. However, I am humble enough to know that every view point, even mine, has its gaps. Its clear that we know what Jesus wants us to know and nothing more. So we have a choice about what we do with the information we are given. A choice to study, a choice to care, or a choice to be complacent and go with the flow. I choose to study and be ready for the future Christ has prepared for his bride. The following paragraphs are suggestions to help believers grasp with what we know and what we do not know or what we cannot understand.

A Mystery We Are Meant to Respect—Knowing in Part, Trusting in Full

If there is one thing we can all agree on when it comes to eschatology, it is this: no one has it all figured out.

The longer you study end-times theology, the more you begin to understand what Jesus meant when he told his disciples, "It is not for you to know times or seasons that the Father has fixed by his own authority" (Acts 1:7). These were men who had walked with Jesus, heard him teach about the kingdom, witnessed his resurrection—and yet, when they asked about restoring the kingdom to Israel, Jesus told them plainly: "That's not for you to know."

But that does not mean they—or we—were meant to be ignorant.

Not Everything Is Hidden

Scripture does not tell us everything about the end times, but it does tell us what we need to know.

It tells us that Jesus will return bodily, visibly, and victoriously.

It tells us there will be a resurrection of the dead, a final judgment, and the creation of a new heaven and new earth.

It tells us that we are to be ready—not with charts but with faithfulness.

And it tells us that the return of Christ is our blessed hope, not a secret puzzle to solve.

We are not meant to be speculative, but we are meant to be informed. We are not called to decode mystery but to live in light of it.

Some people go to one of two extremes when it comes to eschatology:

Overconfidence—They believe they have nailed down every detail. Every prophecy, every timeline, every bowl, trumpet, and seal. They have the charts. They have read the headlines. And often, they speak as if anyone who disagrees is either blind, ignorant, or rebellious.

Apathy—Others throw their hands up and say, "Nobody knows! It will all pan out in the end. Why bother?" They avoid Revelation. They never study the prophets. They see the confusion and decide it is just not worth the effort.

Both positions miss the mark.

The Call to Faithful Curiosity

As believers, we're called to something better: faithful curiosity.

We should care about what Scripture says about the end, not because we think we'll master it but because God put it there for a reason.

When Paul taught the Thessalonians about the return of Christ, he didn't say, "Don't worry about the details." He said, "Encourage one another with these words" (1 Thess 4:18). Eschatology isn't about anxiety—it's about encouragement. It's not about impressing others with our charts but preparing our hearts for our King.

We are not expected to know everything. But we are invited to lean in, to study, to wrestle, to ask good questions, and to hold what we learn with open hands.

That is what this book is—an open-handed attempt to wrestle with God's word honestly and hopefully.

A Call to Humility

Theology, especially eschatology, is not a contest to be won. It is a pursuit of truth. And like every other doctrine, it must be approached with humility and reverence.

What Exactly Is the Millennium?

When Paul reaches the end of Rom 11—a passage filled with mystery, prophecy, and the future of Israel—he does not end with a timeline. He ends with a hymn:

> Oh, the depth of the riches and wisdom and knowledge of God! How unsearchable are his judgments and how inscrutable his ways! (Rom 11:33)

That is how good theology should make us feel—not proud but awed. Not puffed up but worshipful.

If Paul, the greatest theologian of the early church, could reach the limits of his understanding and respond with praise, so should we.

We Do Not Know Everything—but We Know Enough

We don't know when Jesus will return, but we know that he will.

We don't know the full details of what it will look like, but we know we'll be with him (1 Thess 4:17).

We don't know every sign, every sequence, or every symbol, but we know he is coming to judge the living and the dead and to make all things new.

And that is enough to anchor our hope, ignite our mission, and shape our lives.

Eschatology is not just about endings—it's about living faithfully in the middle. It's about enduring suffering, pursuing holiness, preaching the gospel, and keeping our eyes fixed on the horizon.

Do Not Let Mystery Lead to Mistrust

We live in a world that demands certainty. But biblical faith is not the absence of mystery—it's trust in the midst of it.

We do not follow Jesus because we have every question answered. We follow him because he is good, he is risen, and he is coming again.

There is a reason Revelation ends the way it does—not with a chart but with a cry:

> Come, Lord Jesus. (Rev 22:20)

That should be the heartbeat of every believer, regardless of our millennial views. Not "I've figured it out" but "I'm ready to see him."

So What Do We Do?

We study Scripture—not to win debates but to grow in worship.

We hold our views with conviction—but also with charity.

We stay ready—not because we've cracked the code but because we've trusted the king.

We love his appearing. We long for his return. And we live like citizens of a kingdom that is already here—and still on its way.

We don't have all the answers.

We were never supposed to.

But we do have Jesus—and that is enough.

Before we move on to chapter 2, here are some initial observations for consideration:

- Why would the rest of the New Testament speak so little of a literal thousand-year reign if it were central to Christian hope?
- When Jesus said, "My kingdom is not of this world," was he postponing a kingdom—or redefining it?
- If Satan is "bound" now (Rev 20:2–3), how can that be reconciled with his ongoing influence in the world?

The Goal: Humble Curiosity, Not Certainty

This chapter doesn't offer all the answers—it asks you to be open to a new framework. If the millennium in Rev 20 is symbolic, and if Christ is already reigning as King through his resurrection and exaltation, then we might already be living in the time that so many are waiting for.

That is not a view of defeat or denial—it is a view of hope, victory, and purpose. On the following page, you can see a table with a breakdown of these views.

Coming Next

In chapter 2, we will look at the roots of amillennialism—what it teaches, where it came from, and why many people misunderstand it.

Aspect	Dispensational Premillennialism	Historic Premillennialism	Postmillennialism	Amillennialism	Dispensational Amillennialism (Hybrid)
Millennium	Literal thousand-year reign of Christ on earth after his return	Literal thousand-year reign of Christ on earth after his return	Symbolic "golden age" of gospel success before Christ's return	Symbolic current church age; Christ reigns spiritually from heaven	Symbolic current church age; Christ reigns spiritually, no literal thousand-year reign
Christ's Return	Two-stage; pre-tribulation rapture, then second coming after seven-year tribulation.	Single return before the millennium; no pre-tribulation rapture	Single return after a golden age of gospel triumph	Single, climactic return at the end of the church age	Single return at the end of the church age; rapture possible, but not dogmatic.

Millennium in the Middle

Aspect	Dispensational Premillennialism	Historic Premillennialism	Postmillennialism	Amillennialism	Dispensational Amillennialism (Hybrid)
Tribulation	Literal seven-year period of intense global distress before Christ's return	Period of tribulation before Christ's return; duration less defined	Tribulation may occur, but diminishes as gospel transforms world	Ongoing tribulation throughout the church age; may intensify before Christ's return	Literal seven-year tribulation; aligned with Satan's "little while" (Rev 20:3)
Satan's Binding	Future, during the literal millennium; Satan is completely inactive	Future, during the literal millennium; Satan is restrained	Presently bound, allowing gospel to transform the world	Presently bound in a limited sense, preventing total deception of nations	Presently bound in a limited sense; released briefly during tribulation for global deception.
Israel's Role	Distinct from the church; literal restoration in the millennium	Distinct but less emphasis on national restoration; focus on spiritual unity	Promises to Israel fulfilled in the church and global Christianization	Promises to Israel fulfilled in Christ and the church; future Jewish salvation possible	Promises fulfilled in Christ; future Jewish salvation and literal restoration possible

What Exactly Is the Millennium?

Aspect	Dispensational Premillennialism	Historic Premillennialism	Postmillennialism	Amillennialism	Dispensational Amillennialism (Hybrid)
Rapture	Pre-tribulation, secret catching up of the church before the tribulation	No distinct rapture; believers meet Christ at his return	No distinct rapture; focus on gospel progress before return	No distinct rapture; believers meet Christ at his return	Possible pre-tribulation rapture coinciding with Satan's release (Rev 20:3, 7–8) enabling rapid deception of nations; or at Christ's return, not dogmatic
Resurrection	Two resurrections: righteous before millennium, wicked after	Two resurrections: righteous before millennium, wicked after	Single resurrection at Christ's return	Single bodily resurrection at Christ's return; "first resurrection" is spiritual	Single bodily resurrection at Christ's return; "first resurrection" is spiritual

Millennium in the Middle

Aspect	Dispensational Premillennialism	Historic Premillennialism	Postmillennialism	Amillennialism	Dispensational Amillennialism (Hybrid)
Old Testament Prophecies	Literal fulfillment in the millennium (e.g., temple, land promises)	Partial literal fulfilment, some spiritualized in Christ's church	Fulfilled in gospel age and church before Christ's return	Fulfilled in Christ; church and new creation mostly spiritual	Fulfilled in Christ and church; some (e.g., temple) may have literal future aspects

Chapter 2

The Roots of Amillennialism

SAY THE WORD AMILLENNIALISM in a Bible study or seminary classroom and you will likely get mixed reactions—raised eyebrows, head tilts, or maybe a full-on chart war. Some think it sounds like heresy. Others think it sounds like hope. But before we accept or reject it, we need to understand what it is—and what it is not.

Few theological terms are as misleading as the word amillennialism. At face value, it sounds like a denial of the millennium altogether—a rejection of any kind of reign of Christ. But that is not what this view teaches at all. It is not that amillennialists believe there is no millennium—it is that they believe the millennium is now.

In this chapter, we will explore where amillennialism came from, what it teaches, how it has been misunderstood, and why it might make more sense than it first appears.

Let us start by clearing the air.

What Amillennialism Is Not

Amillennialism is often misunderstood as a denial of Christ's future return or a dismissal of God's promises. In reality, it affirms

- the bodily return of Christ,

- the final judgment,
- the resurrection of the dead, and
- the eternal reign of God in the new heaven and new earth.

The "a-" in amillennialism does not mean "no millennium" but rather "not a literal thousand-year future kingdom on earth." Amillennialists believe we are already living in the millennium—a symbolic period between Christ's first and second coming where he reigns spiritually and Satan is bound in a specific, limited way.

To say amillennialism denies the millennium is like saying people who do not believe in a literal beast with ten horns must not believe in evil governments. The issue is not the reality behind the symbol—the issue is how we interpret it.

Amillennialists believe the thousand years mentioned in Rev 20 is a symbolic picture of the current age—the time between Christ's first coming and his second. During this time:

- Christ reigns from heaven,
- Satan is bound from deceiving the nations as he once did, and
- the church advances the gospel under the authority of the risen King.

This interpretation does not ignore prophecy—it reinterprets it in light of the cross, the resurrection, and Pentecost.

The very nature of apocalyptic literature invites us to read symbolically what might not be intended as literal history. If Jesus is not literally a lamb with seven eyes (Rev 5:6), why must the "thousand years" be a literal earthly reign?

Revelation is a book rich in imagery, and any attempt to interpret it must begin with understanding its genre: apocalyptic literature. This genre was never intended to be read like a newspaper or calendar. Instead, it draws heavily from symbols to communicate transcendent truths about God's rule and the battle between good and evil.

Consider the imagery already in Revelation: Jesus is a lamb with seven horns and seven eyes (Rev 5:6). A woman is clothed with the sun (Rev 12:1). A dragon sweeps a third of the stars from the sky (Rev 12:4). Clearly, these are not literal images but theological symbols. And yet, when readers arrive at Rev 20, many suddenly switch to a literal hermeneutic—as if the thousand years must refer to a physical, future timeline.

Amillennial interpreters ask, why change the rules of interpretation midstream?

The "thousand years" is best seen as a symbolic number denoting completeness—a long but definite period in which Christ reigns from heaven and Satan's ability to deceive is curtailed. It is a parallel image to other symbolic numbers in the book (like 144,000 or the seven seals).

Revelation's purpose is not to chart a step-by-step future but to offer a cosmic perspective on present struggles. It gives suffering Christians a vision of ultimate victory, where Jesus reigns even now over the chaos. That's not speculative—it's worship-inducing.

Amillennialism is not a denial of Christ's kingdom—it's a bold affirmation that he reigns now.

A Timeline of Thought: From the Apostles to Today

To understand the strength of amillennialism, we must understand its place in the broader history of Christian interpretation. Contrary to the notion that it is a modern invention, amillennialism has deep roots in the early church and a long-standing influence on Christian theology.

Apostolic Period (First Century)

There is no clear mention of a "millennium" in any of the apostolic writings outside Rev 20. The emphasis in Acts, Romans, and the epistles is on Christ's resurrection, present reign, and imminent return. Paul, for instance, speaks of Jesus already reigning until all enemies are under his feet (1 Cor 15:25).

Early Church Fathers (Second to Fourth Century)

Some like Papias and Justin Martyr held early forms of premillennialism. However, by the third and fourth centuries, influential thinkers, like Origen and especially Augustine, helped move the church toward a symbolic view of Revelation and the "millennium."

The eschatology of the early church did not develop in a vacuum—it was deeply shaped by the pressures of empire. Christians under Roman rule lived in a constant tension between hope and hostility. The *Pax Romana* promised peace, but only through power and persecution. This environment naturally nurtured an apocalyptic imagination.

It's no wonder that early Christian writings, especially Revelation, are filled with vivid imagery of beasts, tyrants, and cosmic battles. To the suffering church, these were not just symbols—they were reflections of real experience. But it also meant that interpretation was often immediate and urgent. The temptation to read prophecy through the lens of present hardship was strong.

As persecution intensified under emperors like Nero and Domitian, some believers leaned into a literal expectation of Christ returning soon to overthrow Rome. This helped fuel early forms of premillennialism. Yet, as the church began to grow and gain stability, especially after Constantine, this literal urgency began to shift.

The turning point came when Christianity was no longer a persecuted minority but a state-supported religion. Suddenly, many began to ask: is the kingdom already here? If so, what do we make of Christ's reign in this new era of imperial peace?

Augustine would eventually answer that question by turning away from earthly expectations. But the Roman backdrop helps us understand how millennial views evolved—not simply from Scripture alone but through the fire of history and persecution.

The Roots of Amillennialism

Augustine and the Medieval Church (Fourth to Fifteenth Century)

Augustine's *The City of God* formalized the idea that the millennium was a spiritual reality, not a future age. This view became the standard interpretation in both the Eastern and Western church for over a millennium (no pun intended).

Consider Augustine's words:

> Those who, on the strength of this passage [Rev 20], have suspected that the first resurrection is future and bodily, have been moved chiefly by the number of a thousand years.... But the truth is, that the church even now is the kingdom of Christ, and the kingdom of heaven. Accordingly, even now His saints reign with Him, though otherwise than as they shall reign hereafter.... The devil is bound now, not that he may not still tempt the saints, but that he may not seduce the nations.[1]

Summary of What Augustine Is Saying

The thousand years is not a literal future period.

The first resurrection is spiritual (conversion/regeneration).

The devil is bound now, not absent but limited in his ability to deceive the nations.

The saints reign now with Christ, not bodily on earth but spiritually in the present age.

The church is the current form of the kingdom—not something delayed until after Christ's return.

Reformation Era (Sixteenth to Seventeenth Century)

The Protestant Reformers, rejecting the Catholic Church's abuses, retained Augustine's eschatology. They upheld a single return of

---

1. Augustine, *City of God*, 20.9.

Christ, a single resurrection, and one final judgment—hallmarks of the amillennial view.

Modern Era (Eighteenth to Twentieth Century)

Dispensationalism gained traction, especially in America, due to the influence of John Nelson Darby, the *Scofield Reference Bible*, and later, the *Left Behind* phenomenon. But amillennialism never disappeared—it quietly persisted in Reformed, Lutheran, and some Anglican traditions.

Today (Twenty-First Century)

Amillennialism is seeing renewed interest, especially among younger evangelicals and Reformed pastors tired of speculative eschatology and eager for a more Christ-centered approach to prophecy.

The Reformation and the Kingdom of Christ

One often overlooked aspect of Reformation theology is its decisive break from the premillennial expectations of early Jewish-Christian apocalypticism. The Reformers did not just recover the doctrine of justification—they recovered a unified view of redemptive history.

While figures like Papias and Justin Martyr held to a literal future reign of Christ, the Reformers returned to the Augustinian understanding of a present spiritual kingdom. They rejected the idea that Christ would return to earth only to rule a thousand-year political kingdom before ushering in eternity.

Why? Because they saw this as a return to Jewish ceremonialism—a physical kingdom with borders, laws, and sacrifices. Luther and Calvin both saw this as a dangerous misreading of the new covenant. Christ fulfilled the types and shadows. To bring back an earthly kingdom was to reverse redemptive progress.

Calvin, especially, warned that such views distracted from the gospel. "It is absurd to expect the Kingdom of God on earth in carnal splendor," he wrote. "Christ's reign is spiritual, not ceremonial or civil."[2] Their rejection of Premillennialism was not casual—it was theological and Christ-centered.

In fact, many Reformers saw premillennialism as bordering on heresy—not because they feared prophecy but because they believed it undermined the finality and sufficiency of Christ's work. The Reformation was a return to Christ alone—not just for salvation but for kingdom, reign, and hope.

When the Reformers challenged Rome, they were not just reforming ecclesiology and soteriology—they were also reclaiming a Christ-centered view of history and the kingdom.

John Calvin

Calvin did not write a full commentary on Revelation (likely because of its symbolic nature), but his view of the kingdom is clear: Christ rules now, through his word and Spirit, and the church lives in the tension of the "already/not yet." Calvin strongly rejected Jewish and earthly interpretations of a future kingdom, arguing for a spiritual and present reign of Christ:

> The kingdom of God is present in the hearts of believers by the Holy Spirit; it is not confined to any earthly or temporal kingdom. The thousand years spoken of by John are to be understood figuratively, describing the current reign of Christ from heaven.[3]

Calvin argued against Jewish or earthly kingdom expectations, seeing the millennium as a symbolic period of Christ's spiritual reign between the first and second comings.

---

2. Calvin, *Institutes*, 4.20.1.
3. Calvin, *Institutes*, 3.25.

Martin Luther

Martin Luther lived in turbulent times and spoke often of the end. But he never adopted a premillennial framework. He emphasized that the word of God, not geopolitical events, was the key to understanding the future. Like Calvin, he expected one climactic return of Christ, not multiple phases:

> The kingdom of Christ is spiritual, and the reign of Christ is the heart which believes in Him.... The thousand years of which John speaks [Rev 20] are not to be taken literally. We are living in the time of the kingdom of Christ, which began with His coming and will continue until the end of the world.[4]

Luther emphasized that Christ's kingdom is a spiritual reign present now, rather than a future earthly political kingdom.

The Confessions

The Westminster Confession, Belgic Confession, and Second Helvetic Confession all reflect a non-millennial framework, affirming the present spiritual reign of Christ and a single, glorious consummation at his return.

Westminster Confession of Faith (1646)

Chapter 8, Section 1—Of Christ the Mediator:

> It pleased God, in His eternal purpose, to choose and ordain the Lord Jesus . . . unto whom He did from all eternity give a people to be His seed, and to be by Him in time redeemed, called, justified, sanctified, and glorified.[5]

---

4. Luther, *Table Talk*, 159.
5. Westminster Assembly, *Westminster Confession*, 8.1.

Chapter 8, Section 4:

> This office the Lord Jesus did most willingly undertake ... and doth continue to exercise it by His intercession for them and revealing unto them, through the Word and Spirit, the will of God in all things concerning their edification and salvation.[6]

Implication: Christ is currently reigning and interceding for his people—not waiting to begin his reign in a future millennial kingdom.

Belgic Confession (1561)

Article 27—The Catholic Christian Church:

> This holy Church is not confined, bound, or limited to a certain place or certain persons, but is spread and dispersed throughout the entire world ... being governed by one only Head, namely, Jesus Christ.[7]

Article 31—The Ministers, Elders, and Deacons:

> We believe that ministers of the Word of God ... are to govern the Church of God according to the spiritual order that our Lord has taught us in His Word.[8]

Implication: Christ governs his church spiritually as its present king, through his word and Spirit, not by means of a future earthly throne.

---

6. Westminster Assembly, *Westminster Confession*, 8.4
7. Christian Reformed Church, *Belgic Confession*, 27.
8. Christian Reformed Church, *Belgic Confession*, 31.

Second Helvetic Confession (1566)

Chapter 11—Of Jesus Christ, True God and Man, the Only Savior of the World:

> We further believe and teach that the same Jesus Christ our Lord ... now sits at the right hand of God the Father, and yet is with us unto the end of the world ... governing all things with the Father.[9]

Chapter 11 also says, "Christ is truly reigning now from heaven and effectually works in His people."[10]

Chapter 19—Of the Church

> The Church is governed by the Word and Spirit of Christ, and not by any earthly hierarchy.[11]

Implication: Christ's reign is a present spiritual reign over his church from heaven—not something postponed until after his return.

These confessions explicitly reject a postponed or earthly political kingdom in favor of a present, spiritual reign of Christ—the very heart of amillennial theology.

Who's Teaching This Today?

Amillennialism is not just an academic artifact—it is a living, taught, and preached view held by thoughtful and biblically faithful voices today. Before you think this idea is just held by a few, or an idea of the past, consider who is teaching this today. Read from their own voices! Here are a few notable examples:

---

9. Christian Reformed Church, *Second Helvetic Confession*, 11.
10. Christian Reformed Church, *Second Helvetic Confession*, 11.
11. Christian Reformed Church, *Second Helvetic Confession*, 19.

Kim Riddlebarger

Pastor, theologian, and author of *A Case for Amillennialism*, Riddlebarger writes,

> The millennium is the period of time between the two advents of our Lord, with the thousand years of Revelation 20 being symbolic of the entire interadvental age.[12]

Anthony Hoekema

Late Reformed theologian, whose book *The Bible and the Future* remains a respected amillennial work, Hoekema wrote,

> The book of Revelation, therefore, pictures the church of Jesus Christ as saved, secure in Christ, and destined for future glory—yet as still subject to suffering and persecution while the bridegroom tarries.[13]

Sam Storms

A Continuationism theologian who identifies as amillennial and brings fresh pastoral insight, Storms writes,

> My conclusion is that when we examine what the New Testament says will occur at the time of the second coming/advent of Jesus Christ, there is no place for a 1,000 year earthly reign to follow. At the time of the second coming there will occur the final resurrection, the final judgment, the end of sin, the end of death, and the creation of the new heavens and new earth.[14]

---

12. Riddlebarger, *Case for Amillennialism*, 94.
13. Hoekema, *Amillennialism*, 110.
14. Storms, *Kingdom Come*, 165.

Michael Horton

A systematic theologian at Westminster Seminary California with a strong amillennial perspective, Horton writes,

> We are living in the period described symbolically in Revelation 20 as a thousand-year reign of Christ, to be followed by Christ's return.... What we reject is a literalistic interpretation of the thousand years, since the book of Revelation employs numbers symbolically.[15]

R. C. Sproul

Sproul often leaned toward amillennial or partial preterist positions and encouraged gracious dialogue:

> The millennium is the period in which Christ reigns now from heaven, reigning over His church and restraining the power of Satan until the final consummation when He returns visibly and gloriously.[16]

John Piper

John Piper identifies himself with historic premillennialism, yet he consistently demonstrates humility and collegiality in discussing other eschatological positions. In a roundtable discussion, he said he regards amillennialism as the "next most plausible view." He also affirms that the "thousand years" in Rev 20 could be symbolic, representing a prolonged age of Christ's heavenly reign, and holds that the millennium begins after Christ's return—which means, in his words, "Christ could come very, very quickly."[17]

---

15. Horton, *Introducing Covenant Theology*, 120.
16. Sproul, *Last Days According to Jesus*, 226.
17. The "plausible view" comes from Piper, "An Evening of Eschatology," 1:01:25.

Voddie Baucham

A prominent preacher and theologian who affirms amillennialism within a strong exegetical and pastoral framework, Baucham says,

> Amillennialism teaches that the millennium is the present reality, the time between Christ's first and second coming, where He reigns spiritually and the church advances His kingdom until He returns.[18]

These are preachers, teachers, seminary professors, and scholars who all have concluded that this single passage about the millennial reign of Christ is meant to be taken as symbolic. While you should come up with your own conclusion, these voices of the past and present are at least worth considering!

A Kingdom Now—and Not Yet

Amillennialism rests heavily on the idea that Jesus inaugurated his kingdom at his first coming. He declared, "The kingdom of God is at hand" (Mark 1:15). He said, "If I cast out demons by the Spirit of God, then the kingdom of God has come upon you" (Matt 12:28).

Rather than seeing the kingdom as postponed, amillennialism sees it as present but incomplete. Christ reigns now from heaven, and his people—empowered by the Spirit—are part of his kingdom mission on earth. But the full visible consummation of his reign is still to come.

Why Is This View So Misunderstood?

- It is not chart-friendly.
- It does not fit the American evangelical mold.
- It embraces tension.
- The name itself is confusing.

18. Baucham, *When Is the Millennium?*

- It lacks the "wow" factor.
- It is associated with liberal theology.

Is Amillennialism "Replacement Theology"?

One of the major objections to amillennialism is that it seems to erase national Israel from God's future plans. But this misunderstands the view. Amillennialism does not deny God's promises to Israel—it reinterprets them in light of Christ.

Paul makes this clear in Rom 9–11. He does not speak of two separate peoples with two distinct destinies but of one olive tree into which gentiles are grafted. The mystery revealed in the gospel is not that God abandoned Israel but that the gentiles have been included in the people of promise.

The land, temple, and throne promises were never ends in themselves—they pointed forward to Jesus. He is the true temple (John 2:21), the greater Davidic King (Luke 1:32–33), and the One who inherits the nations (Ps 2). As such, amillennialism sees the church not as a replacement but as the expansion of God's covenant people in Christ.

This does not erase Jewish identity or hope. Romans 11 hints at a future ingathering of Jewish people into Christ, which amillennialists affirm. But it locates that hope within the unified people of God, not a separate ethnic plan. The gospel is not two stories—it's one story with one Savior, one cross, and one resurrection for all who believe.

This accusation is common—but inaccurate. Amillennialism does not teach that the church replaces Israel. It teaches that the promises to Israel are fulfilled in Christ and shared with all who are in him (Jew and gentile alike).

Paul says as much in Gal 3:29: "If you are Christ's, then you are Abraham's offspring, heirs according to promise."

This is not erasure. It is expansion. The mystery hidden for ages is that gentiles are now fellow heirs (Eph 3:6). God has one people, not two; one covenant, not two; one future, not two. This will be covered in greater detail in a future chapter.

A Word to Pastors: The Cost of Changing Your View

One of the most underestimated strengths of amillennialism is its pastoral clarity. While other views often spark speculation, timelines, and endless debates over signs, amillennialism redirects attention to the present responsibilities of discipleship.

If Christ reigns now, then how we live today truly matters. If Satan is bound in a real but limited way, then missions is not optional—it's urgent. If we are already seated with Christ in heavenly places (Eph 2:6), then the church isn't just waiting—it's participating in the kingdom now.

This theology gives courage to pastors in small, struggling churches. It comforts believers in persecuted countries. It reminds Western Christians that the goal is not political dominance or cultural victory—but faithfulness.

Pastor Jerry Uchechukwu Eze, a Nigerian pastor, shared a profound experience during a church service in Zambia. He recounted how thousands of believers gathered, some climbing trees and rooftops, to witness a powerful move of God. In his testimony, he emphasized that the reign of Jesus is not a distant hope but a present reality that empowers believers to endure and overcome life's challenges. He stated, "Jesus reigns. . . . I haven't recovered yet."[19]

Amillennialism does not diminish hope. It roots hope in the already-present reign of Christ, while still longing for his return. It frees us from paranoia, from watching the news like prophecy fulfillment bingo, and reorients us to worship, witness, and waiting.

Theology is not just about truth—it is about timing, tone, and trust. For many pastors, embracing amillennialism can be costly.

---

19. Eze, "Jesus Reigns."

Sam Storms lost members when he went public. Mike Abendroth had fellow pastors question his orthodoxy. Even R. C. Sproul, revered as he was, received backlash for leaning away from a literal millennium.

A pastor in rural Texas reported that when he shared his belief that Christ would not reign on earth for a literal thousand years, some members of his congregation assumed he had become liberal. As a result, he lost members—not over faith in Jesus but over disagreement about the timing of Christ's reign.

He did not change his view overnight. He preached the kingdom through Acts, Daniel, and Revelation. He showed them Christ, not charts. And though some left, others stayed—and grew.

Pastoral Advice:

- Preach the Bible, not the label.
- Let Scripture shape your people slowly.
- Expect resistance, but do not fear it.
- Do not lose sight of the gospel.

If this view exalts Christ, fuels your preaching, and aligns with Scripture—it is worth it.

A Personal Note

You may not be convinced yet—and that is okay. But I hope you are at least beginning to see that amillennialism is not the boogeyman it has sometimes made out to be. It has a long history, thoughtful defenders, and deep biblical convictions. In the chapters ahead, we will dig deeper into its specific claims and how it engages with dispensational ideas—not to argue for its superiority but to open our hearts and Bibles to a perspective that might just surprise us.

I once believed that every view except premillennialism was heresy. No good Southern Baptist or Protestant dared believe in anything else. Then when I learned there were indeed other viewpoints, I did not think I would ever adhere to it. I used to think amillennialism was just a cop-out—something people believed when they did not want to deal with prophecy. But as I studied Scripture more deeply, I began to see that it was not shallow—it was simple—not simplistic but elegantly rooted in the finished work of Christ.

I saw how much of the Bible's language about the kingdom, resurrection, judgment, and restoration made more sense when I read Rev 20 in context—not as a puzzle but as a proclamation.

I did not adopt amillennialism because it was easier. I adopted it because I began to see how it made everything else in Scripture come alive with consistency.

With that said, there are personal heroes of mine with whom I disagree, such as Dr. David Jeremiah, John MacArthur, and Skip Heitzig, whom I all love dearly. I frequently listen to their teaching, preaching, and even read their books. However, I, like many others, disagree with them on this single issue. If this chapter has taught you anything, I hope you have learned that it's OK to disagree, and that different eschatological viewpoints are not heretical viewpoints.

Why This Matters for Everyday Believers

You might wonder, why does all this matter? Why should the average Christian care whether Christ reigns now or in some future earthly millennium? Isn't this just for theologians?

The answer is simple: what you believe about the end shapes how you live in the present.

If the kingdom of God is already here in a real, though incomplete, way, then your ordinary acts of obedience—your parenting, your worship, your work, your suffering—are not just fillers before the real action begins. They are part of the kingdom unfolding. You are not just waiting; you are participating.

Amillennialism gives believers a robust theology of hope without escapism. It tells the persecuted believer in China, "Christ reigns even now." It tells the overwhelmed mother in the suburbs, "You are part of God's advancing kingdom." It tells the aging saint in the nursing home, "Your labor is not in vain."

By contrast, an overfocus on a future millennium can unintentionally delay hope. It implies that real victory, real peace, and real justice must wait for some geopolitical future event. But the New Testament insists the power of the age to come has already broken in (Heb 6:5). The Spirit has already been poured out. The King is already on his throne.

That's not just theology—it's fuel for discipleship. It reframes how we suffer, how we serve, and how we see the world.

Conclusion: Ancient, Biblical, and Still Relevant

Amillennialism is not a modern theory. It is a rich, time-tested, Christ-centered framework for understanding the end times. It invites us to live as kingdom people now, while longing for the day when faith becomes sight.

In the next chapter, we will tackle the core of the millennium debate: Rev 20. What does it mean that Satan is bound—and how can that possibly be true right now?

Chapter 3

Satan Bound?
A Closer Look at Revelation 20

THIS CHAPTER FOCUSES ON the meaning of Satan being "bound" in Rev 20:1–3, especially in the context of amillennialism. The key issue isn't whether Satan is completely inactive but whether he is *limited in a specific way* during the millennium.

What Does Revelation 20 Actually Say?
The Text Itself

> Then I saw an angel coming down from heaven, holding in his hand the key to the bottomless pit and a great chain. And he seized the dragon, that ancient serpent, who is the devil and Satan, and bound him for a thousand years, and threw him into the pit, and shut it and sealed it over him, so that he might not deceive the nations any longer, until the thousand years were ended. After that he must be released for a little while. (Rev 20:1–3 ESV)

Let's observe some key features of this passage.

Satan Is Bound, Not Eliminated

First, notice that the passage does *not* say Satan is destroyed, removed from existence, or rendered completely powerless. It says he is *bound* (Greek: *ēdēsen*), which implies a restraint, not annihilation. This distinction is crucial. The language used here is not about total inactivity but *limited ability*.

This binding is *symbolized* by a chain, a key, and a sealed pit. Revelation is a book steeped in symbolic imagery—dragons, beasts, bowls, and thrones all speak of realities behind the veil. We would never claim Satan is literally a dragon or that Christ is literally a lamb standing with blood dripping on a throne. So why, then, would we insist the chain and pit must be woodenly literal?

The *purpose* of Satan's binding is also given: "So that he might not deceive the nations any longer." That is a narrow, specific restriction—not a total shutdown of satanic activity. Satan still prowls like a roaring lion (1 Pet 5:8). He still tempts, accuses, and resists the saints. But he cannot do **one thing**: deceive the nations as he did before the resurrection of Christ.

What the Binding Does Not Mean

There are three critical clarifications needed here:

1. **It does not mean Satan is inactive.**

   He still opposes believers. Spiritual warfare is still real. Revelation itself later shows that demonic forces still influence false religion and worldly systems (see Rev 13 and 17).

2. **It does not mean evil disappears.**

   The presence of evil in the world is not in conflict with the claim that Satan is bound. Evil men, corrupted systems, and personal sin continue even while the devil's strategic influence over the *nations* is curtailed.

3. **It does not mean we live in a utopia.**

A common objection is, "How can we say Satan is bound when the world is so dark?" But this objection misunderstands what Rev 20 actually says. The point of Satan's binding is not to create a golden age but to remove his unique power to blind the nations from the truth of the gospel.

The Premillennial Acknowledgment of Evil

Ironically, even **premillennialists** acknowledge that *evil still exists* during their future millennial reign. According to many premillennial interpretations, Jesus will reign visibly from Jerusalem over a partially redeemed earth for a thousand years. Yet even during this time—when Satan is supposedly bound—*there will still be sinners* who feign obedience, and at the end of the thousand years, Satan will be loosed and gather a final rebellion (Rev 20:7–9).

Let that sink in: even in a literal, earthly millennium *with Satan bound, Christ visibly present*, and glorified saints with him, evil still exists.

So if a *premillennial hermeneutic* allows for evil, rebellion, and opposition during their version of Satan's binding, why would it be considered "impossible" or "naïve" to believe that Satan could be bound *now*—not in every way, but in the way Rev 20 specifically says?

The problem, then, is not *that amillennialism teaches Satan is bound* but that we must be clear *in what way* he is bound. Revelation 20 does not describe a utopia; it describes a spiritual reality in which Satan no longer has the ability to hold the nations in darkness.

Key Terms and Imagery

- **The Bottomless Pit (Abyss):** This is not hell (Gehenna), but a holding place—used elsewhere in Revelation for temporary restraint (e.g., demons in Rev 9). Satan is confined, not extinguished.

- **A Great Chain:** Symbolic of God's authority to limit spiritual beings, Jude 6 speaks of angels kept in "eternal chains" until judgment—clearly symbolic of restraint, not physical chains.
- **Sealed Over Him:** Finality. Until God's timing is fulfilled, Satan cannot break loose or resume global deception.

Conclusion of the Specific Binding

So what does Rev 20 actually say?

- Satan is bound *for a purpose*, not in every sense.
- His binding is symbolic of *a divine restraint*, not destruction.
- The purpose is to prevent him from *deceiving the nations* during the millennium.
- This matches exactly what began at Christ's resurrection and continues through the gospel age.
- Even premillennialists allow for **evil** *during Satan's binding*, which confirms that total inactivity is not required by any consistent hermeneutic.

This clears the path for the next section, where we'll examine the *New Testament witness* to this reality—that Satan's decisive defeat and limitation has already begun.

Scriptural Support for a Present Binding

Revelation 20 says Satan is bound "so that he might not deceive the nations any longer." But can we find evidence for this elsewhere in the New Testament? Absolutely. And not only that—we find *consistent, explicit testimony* that something decisive happened to Satan during Christ's first coming.

The idea that Satan has already been bound in a specific way is not speculative—it's deeply rooted in the ministry of Jesus and the teaching of the apostles. Let's examine the clearest texts supporting this view.

Jesus Declares Satan Bound: Matthew 12:29

> Or how can someone enter a strong man's house and plunder his goods, unless he first binds the strong man? Then indeed he may plunder his house. (Matt 12:29)

In this often-overlooked passage, Jesus uses a parable to explain his authority over demons. He compares himself to a thief entering a strong man's house. But before he can take anything, he must *first bind* the strong man. That's Satan.

The Greek word used here (*deo*, "to bind") is the same word used in Rev 20. Jesus is saying that *his victory over demons is the result of having already bound Satan*. This binding isn't future—it was active during his earthly ministry.

Jesus plunders the devil's kingdom every time he casts out demons, heals the oppressed, or saves a soul. The strong man is bound—not destroyed, not silenced forever, but *restrained* so that Christ's kingdom mission can go forward.

Satan Cast Out: John 12:31-32

> Now is the judgment of this world; now will the ruler of this world be cast out. And I, when I am lifted up from the earth, will draw all people to myself.

These words are spoken by Jesus just before his crucifixion. He does *not* say that Satan will be cast out at some distant point in the future. He says it is happening *now*—through his death.

The "ruler of this world," Satan, is being dethroned. And in his place, Jesus will draw all people to himself—Jews and gentiles, men and women from every nation. The casting out of Satan corresponds directly to the *opening of the gospel to the nations*.

Public Defeat: Colossians 2:15

> He disarmed the rulers and authorities and put them to open shame, by triumphing over them in him.

Paul describes Christ's crucifixion and resurrection not only as redemptive but also as *military*. The cross wasn't just a payment for sin—it was a public *defeat of the powers of darkness*. Satan and his demonic hosts were disarmed, exposed, and humiliated.

This is not future tense. Paul writes of a *past victory*, already accomplished. How could Satan still be deceiving the nations with unchecked power if he's already been publicly stripped of his weapons?

This verse is an unmistakable parallel to Rev 20. In both cases, Satan's influence is curtailed by Christ's redemptive act.

Satan Falls Like Lightning: Luke 10:17–18

> The seventy-two returned with joy, saying, "Lord, even the demons are subject to us in your name!" And he said to them, "I saw Satan fall like lightning from heaven."

Here again, Jesus testifies to a *real-time shift in Satan's authority*. As his disciples preach and heal in his name, Satan's grip is breaking. Jesus sees Satan's fall not in a distant apocalyptic vision but *in response to present gospel ministry*.

This fits perfectly with the idea that Satan's fall and binding are not future events but realities set in motion by Christ's ministry and mission.

Satan's Dominion Broken: Hebrews 2:14–15

> Since therefore the children share in flesh and blood, he himself likewise partook of the same things, that through death he might destroy the one who has the power of death, that is, the devil, and deliver all those who through fear of death were subject to lifelong slavery.

This stunning passage gives deep theological weight to Christ's incarnation and crucifixion. Jesus took on flesh so that *through death*, He might *destroy the devil's power and free those enslaved by fear and darkness*.

This is the very definition of what Rev 20 means by Satan being bound "so that he might not deceive the nations any longer." His grip over humanity—rooted in fear, condemnation, and death—was *broken by Christ's sacrifice*.

Satan still exists, and he still tempts, but he no longer reigns over the nations as he once did. The cross didn't merely offer salvation—it unleashed a spiritual revolution.

The Nations Now See: Acts 26:17-18

> I am sending you to open their eyes, so that they may turn from darkness to light and from the power of Satan to God.

These are the words Jesus spoke to Paul at his commissioning. The gospel ministry Paul is called to will literally *deliver the nations from Satan's power*. The work of missions is described as moving people *out of Satan's dominion* into God's kingdom.

This aligns perfectly with Rev 20:3—Satan is bound in such a way that he can no longer deceive the nations wholesale. Wherever the gospel is preached, his grip is broken.

Passage	Timing	Satan's Condition
Matt 12:29	During Jesus' ministry	Bound so Christ can plunder souls
John 12:31	At the cross	Cast out from global rule
Col 2:15	At the cross	Disarmed and publicly shamed
Luke 10:18	During gospel mission	Fallen like lightning
Heb 2:14-15	At the cross	Destroyed death's dominion
Acts 26:18	Ongoing mission	Nations freed from Satan's power

Conclusion: The Present Binding Is Biblically Grounded

Taken together, these Scriptures form a powerful argument: *Satan is already bound*, and the binding began with Christ's first coming. This is not a marginal interpretation—it's the clear message of Jesus, Paul, and the early church.

Of course, there are *other passages*—such as **Rev 12**—that many scholars and pastors believe also support this view. However, since their timing and interpretation are debated, I have intentionally left them out of this chapter in order to build on *ground we all can agree on*: Satan's defeat and limitation is a central and celebrated theme of the New Testament.

In the next section, we'll explore the *results* of this binding. What changed when Satan lost his grip on the nations? What new reality began to dawn?

What Did Satan's Binding Accomplish?

If Rev 20 tells us that Satan was bound so that he could no longer deceive the nations, and if the New Testament confirms that this binding began at Christ's first coming, then we must ask, *What did this accomplish in real terms?*

The answer is profound: Satan's defeat opened the floodgates of salvation to the nations. What was once a world dominated by idolatry, paganism, and spiritual darkness has now been radically transformed by the light of the gospel. The binding of Satan didn't bring an end to evil—but it *ended the monopoly* he held over the world.

Before the Resurrection: Nations in Darkness

The Old Testament portrays a world largely *cut off from the knowledge of God*. Only Israel had the Scriptures, the covenants, the promises, and the revealed worship of Yahweh.

He declares his word to Jacob, his statutes and rules to Israel. He has not dealt thus with any other nation. (Ps 147:19–20)

The gentile world was steeped in idolatry, sorcery, and spiritual blindness. Paul vividly describes this in Ephesians:

You were dead in the trespasses and sins in which you once walked, following the course of this world, following the prince of the power of the air. (Eph 2:1–2)

The *nations were deceived*, following demonic spirits (1 Cor 10:20) and suppressing the truth (Rom 1:18–32). But then something changed.

After Christ's Resurrection: The Nations Awaken

When Christ rose from the dead and ascended to heaven, Satan was bound, and the mission to *disciple the nations* began.

Go therefore and make disciples of all nations. (Matt 28:19)

This Great Commission was not just a new command—it was a *cosmic breakthrough*. For the first time in history, the nations were no longer under Satan's exclusive influence. The church, filled with the Spirit, now had divine power to go to every tribe, tongue, and language.

He has delivered us from the domain of darkness and transferred us to the kingdom of his beloved Son. (Col 1:13)

This is precisely the effect Rev 20 anticipates: Satan is bound so that the nations could be *delivered from deception and brought into the light of Christ*.

Millennium in the Middle

Historical Testimony: From Jerusalem to the Ends of the Earth

From a small group of Galilean disciples, the gospel began to spread like wildfire. Consider this sweeping historical timeline:

- **First through third centuries**: Despite fierce Roman persecution, the church spreads across North Africa, the Middle East, and Southern Europe. Tertullian wrote that Christians filled "every place in the empire."

- **Fourth century**: Emperor Constantine converts, and Christianity becomes legal throughout the Roman Empire.

- **Sixth through tenth centuries**: Missionaries such as St. Patrick (Ireland), St. Augustine of Canterbury (England), and Cyril and Methodius (Slavic lands) carry the gospel to unreached peoples.

- **Fifteenth through seventeenth centuries**: The Reformation leads to massive translation and dissemination of the Bible—Luther, Tyndale, Calvin, and others turn the light back on in Europe.

- **Eighteenth through twentieth centuries**: The Modern Missions Movement explodes: William Carey to India, Hudson Taylor to China, Adoniram Judson to Burma. By the 1900s, evangelical missions had reached every continent.

What could possibly explain such massive global transformation *except* that the "strong man" was bound?

The Bible: From One Nation to Every Nation

One of the most striking pieces of evidence of Satan's binding is the *unprecedented availability of the Bible*. What was once limited to Hebrew scrolls in synagogues is now everywhere.

Satan Bound?

As of 2024 (according to Wycliffe Global Alliance and the YouVersion Bible app):[1]

- the full Bible is available in **736 languages**
- the New Testament is available in an additional **1,658 languages**
- portions of Scripture exist in over **3,600 languages**
- more than **95 percent of the world's population** has access to the Bible in a language they understand

By comparison, just *five hundred years ago*, virtually *no one outside Europe* had access to a full printed Bible. Today, the Bible is in your pocket, on your phone, online, in audio, video, and print—in nearly every language.

This isn't accidental. It is a *fulfillment of Jesus' promise* that the gospel would be preached to all nations—and it would not be possible if Satan were still free to blind them all.

Dreams, Visions, and Gospel Breakthroughs Among Muslims

Another striking evidence of Satan's diminished influence is the remarkable number of *Muslims coming to Christ*, especially through dreams and visions.

In regions where Christianity is outlawed and Satan has long held sway, Jesus is still reaching people:

- In Iran, Christianity is growing *faster than in any other nation* in the world. House churches have exploded despite persecution.
- In countries like Egypt, Syria, and Saudi Arabia, there are *countless testimonies* of Muslims seeing Jesus in dreams and being led to believers or missionaries.

---

1. Wycliffe Global Alliance, "2024 Global Scripture Access."

- A 2007 study by Fuller Theological Seminary found that **25 percent of Muslim-background believers** cited dreams or visions as a key factor in their conversion.

These testimonies are not isolated. Entire networks of underground churches are forming in places that were once strongholds of deception. Why? Because the strong man is *bound*, and Christ is plundering his house—even in the most resistant cultures.

The Work Is Not Finished, but the Walls Are Down

None of this means that Satan has given up. He still deceives individuals, foments false religions, and persecutes the saints. But *his ability to hold the nations in total darkness has been broken.*

Missionaries now travel freely.

Scripture circulates globally.

People from every tribe and tongue are hearing the gospel.

And even where persecution is fierce, the gospel still advances. The blood of the martyrs has become the seed of the church.

This is what it means for Satan to be bound—not silence, not absence, but *restraint from the power he once wielded freely* over the gentile nations.

Conclusion: The Binding of Satan Was a Global Turning Point

- The nations were once blind, deceived, and enslaved.
- Christ came, died, rose, and ascended—and Satan's grip broke.
- The gospel spread across the world.
- The Bible is in almost every language.
- Muslims are coming to Christ through dreams and visions.
- Satan is still active, but he is *not in control*.

This is exactly what Rev 20 means when it says Satan was bound "so that he might not deceive the nations any longer." It is not a utopia. It is a *mission field where victory is now possible*.

Next, we'll answer a pressing question: if Satan is bound, why does it still feel like he's so active in the world? How do we reconcile that with Rev 20?

Objection: Isn't Satan Still Active?

One of the most common objections to the amillennial understanding of Rev 20 is this: *"If Satan is bound, how do you explain the evil in the world? What about the demonic, false religions, persecution, and spiritual warfare? Isn't that proof he's still free and active?"*

This are serious and honest questions. The world is clearly not free of evil. Christians suffer. Spiritual deception abounds. Satan is still at work.

But here is the key: *Rev 20 never says Satan is inactive. It says he is restricted in one specific way.* Let us unpack what that means.

Revelation 20 Limits Satan's Binding to One Purpose

> So that he might not deceive the nations any longer, until the thousand years were ended. (Rev 20:3)

The *"so that" clause* in this verse tells us exactly what kind of binding is being described. It's not total immobilization. It's not the removal of all satanic influence. It is a *targeted restraint*: Satan is bound *so that he can no longer deceive the nations* in the way he once did.

This doesn't mean he can't tempt individuals.

It doesn't mean he can't promote lies.

It doesn't mean the church won't face spiritual opposition.

It means he can no longer blind entire people groups from the truth. The nations, once enveloped in darkness, are now accessible to the gospel.

Scripture Confirms Satan Is Active, Yet Limited

Even after Jesus binds Satan (Matt 12:29), the New Testament still warns believers about the devil's schemes. This is no contradiction—it's consistent with *limited activity.*

Here are just a few examples:

- **1 Pet 5:8**—"Your adversary the devil prowls around like a roaring lion, seeking someone to devour."
- **Jas 4:7**—"Resist the devil, and he will flee from you."
- **2 Cor 11:14**—"Satan disguises himself as an angel of light."
- **Eph 6:11-12**—"Put on the whole armor of God ... to stand against the schemes of the devil."

These warnings are not evidence that Satan is free to deceive the nations as before; they are *reminders that personal temptation and spiritual warfare continue,* even while the broader power of global deception has been curtailed.

The Strong Man Analogy Again

Remember Jesus' parable in Matt 12:29:

> How can someone enter a strong man's house and plunder his goods, unless he first binds the strong man?

Jesus didn't say the strong man (Satan) was tied up in a soundproof closet. He's *bound* but still in the house. And Christ is plundering it—saving souls, reclaiming hearts, breaking chains.

Satan can still growl. He can still deceive individuals. But he *cannot stop* the mission of the gospel.

Satan Bound?

Even Premillennialists Admit Evil Exists During the Millennium

Here is an often-overlooked irony: Even those who insist on a *future, literal millennium* agree that *evil still exists during that time*—even while Satan is bound.

In most dispensational views, the millennial kingdom will include

- people born with sinful natures,
- hypocrites who outwardly obey but inwardly rebel, and
- a final rebellion at the end of the thousand years when Satan is released (Rev 20:7–9)

So even in their framework, *Satan's binding does not require the absence of sin or evil.*

That means the amillennial view—which sees Satan as bound now but evil still present—is actually *more consistent* than many realize. It takes the text at face value without demanding unrealistic conditions.

Satan Is on a Leash

Think of Satan like a vicious dog on a chain. If you get too close, you'll get bitten. But he can't roam freely. He's *limited by the chain*, restrained by God's authority.

The book of Job gives us a picture of Satan on a leash—he must *ask permission* to afflict Job (Job 1:6–12). In Luke 22:31, Jesus says,

> Simon, Simon, Satan has asked to sift all of you as wheat.

Satan has designs, but he needs *divine permission*. His power is neither sovereign nor unrestrained. That has always been true, and now, because of the cross, it's even more so.

The Gospel Keeps Advancing

If Satan were still free to deceive the nations as he once did, the spread of the gospel would be impossible. But we have already seen

- the Bible is in over 3,600 languages,
- missionaries have reached nearly every people group,
- Muslims are coming to Christ in record numbers, and
- entire regions once hostile to Christianity are now home to thriving churches.

These are not the works of a world held under satanic deception. These are the fruits of Christ's victory—and Satan's limitation.

Application: Victory, Not Fear

Understanding the restrained role of Satan should not lead us to complacency but to *confidence*.

Yes, the devil still prowls.

Yes, we still face spiritual warfare.

But the outcome is secure. Christ reigns. The gospel marches on. And Satan's defeat is not only promised—it is already *in motion*.

As Paul reminds us,

> The God of peace will soon crush Satan under your feet. (Rom 16:20)

Not "might." Not "someday far off." *Soon.* Because the victory has already begun.

Conclusion: A Bound Yet Roaring Enemy

- Satan is bound from deceiving the nations, not from opposing individuals.
- Scripture confirms his ongoing but *limited* activity.

- Even premillennial frameworks allow for evil during Satan's binding.
- The gospel's global advance is living proof that his power has been curtailed.

In the next section, we'll examine what this all means for our understanding of the millennium. If Satan is bound now, could it be that the "thousand years" has already begun?

A Present, Spiritual Millennium

Much confusion surrounding Rev 20 stems from expectations that the millennium must be a golden age—an earthly paradise, free from sin, suffering, or spiritual opposition.

But the text itself doesn't promise that.

Revelation 20 describes a reign—a rule of Christ in which Satan is restrained, the saints are victorious, and the gospel goes forth to the nations. It never says this period will be free of pain or have perfect peace. In fact, a sober reading of the passage within the larger biblical narrative points to something deeper and more profound.

The Millennium Is Christ's Present, Spiritual Reign Over All Creation

Christ Reigns Now

The New Testament makes this claim repeatedly. Christ is not waiting to reign—he is *already enthroned.*

> All authority in heaven and on earth has been given to me. (Matt 28:18)

> He must reign until he has put all enemies under his feet. (1 Cor 15:25)

> God . . . seated him at his right hand in the heavenly realms, far above all rule and authority. (Eph 1:20–21)

These are not promises about a future government headquartered in Jerusalem. These are *current realities*. Christ reigns *now*—from heaven, over all powers and authorities. His kingdom is not limited by borders or politics. It is *invisible, eternal*, and *spiritually present* in the world.

The Kingdom We Cannot See—but Truly Belong To

Jesus taught that his kingdom was unlike anything people expected. When asked by Pilate if he was a king, Jesus responded,

> My kingdom is not of this world. (John 18:36)

He wasn't denying his kingship—he was *redefining it*. His reign would not be through armies but through the gospel. His power would not be measured in politics but in changed hearts.

Paul echoes this:

> The kingdom of God is not a matter of eating and drinking but of righteousness and peace and joy in the Holy Spirit. (Rom 14:17)

And again:

> He has delivered us from the domain of darkness and transferred us to the kingdom of his beloved Son. (Col 1:13)

The millennium is not a time when Christ *will* reign—it is the age in which Christ *is reigning*, even if we cannot yet see all the outward signs. Like the wind, we can't see the kingdom directly, but we know it's real by its effects: people being saved, churches growing, and lives being transformed.

Living in the Already/Not Yet

The New Testament writers lived with this tension: *Christ reigns now, yet the world is not yet fully restored.* They were not waiting for a utopia—they were bearing witness to a *hidden kingdom* breaking into a broken world.

The apostle John, who wrote Revelation, says,

> I, John, your brother and partner in the tribulation and the kingdom and the patient endurance that are in Jesus. (Rev 1:9o)

John does not say, "We're waiting for the kingdom." He says, "I'm your *partner in it*—right now." And this kingdom comes *with tribulation*, not just triumph. It's a reign *amid suffering*, not the absence of it.

The First Resurrection: A Spiritual Reality

One of the main arguments for a future millennium is Rev 20's mention of a *"first resurrection."* But notice how John describes those who share in it:

> Blessed and holy is the one who shares in the first resurrection! Over such the second death has no power. (Rev 20:6)

What is the "first resurrection"? It is *spiritual*—the new birth, regeneration, the moment when a person passes from death to life in Christ. Paul writes,

> Even when we were dead in our trespasses, [God] made us alive together with Christ. (Eph 2:5)

This is the resurrection of *souls*, not bodies—those who have been spiritually awakened and who reign with Christ now. Later in the chapter, the *second resurrection* is physical (at the final judgment). This reinforces the idea that the millennium is spiritual—not earthly or physical.

The Testimony of the Apostles and Early Church

The apostles lived with the firm belief that they were already part of Christ's reigning kingdom, even though they were persecuted, poor, and opposed. Paul calls believers "seated with him in the heavenly places in Christ Jesus" (Eph 2:6).

Even while imprisoned, Paul rejoices in Christ's kingship. Even while beaten, he proclaims Jesus as *Lord of all*.

Early Christians held the same view. They did not fear death because they believed they had already *entered into Christ's kingdom*. Tertullian, writing around AD 200, said,

> The kingdom of God is promised to believers even in the present time, although it is yet hidden.[2]

Polycarp, a disciple of John, went to his death by fire refusing to deny Christ, not because he hoped Jesus would *one day reign* but because he *knew he already did*.

The courage of the martyrs wasn't rooted in a coming utopia—it was grounded in the certainty that *Jesus is already enthroned*, and they were already reigning with him spiritually, even in suffering.

We Are the Children of the Kingdom

Jesus said, "Fear not, little flock, for it is your Father's good pleasure to give you the kingdom" (Luke 12:32).

That kingdom is not a future estate in Palestine—it's a present inheritance for all who belong to Jesus.

To say the millennium has begun is not to deny evil, pain, or persecution. It is to *proclaim that Christ reigns anyway*. It is to live under his rule, even when the world around us seems to rebel.

The glory of the millennium is not perfect peace but *perfect governance*—that *Jesus rules now*, and his saints, whether on earth or in heaven, are already his kingdom people.

---

2. Tertullian, *Apologeticus*, 3.

Satan Bound?

Conclusion: The Millennium Is Here—and Christ Reigns

- The millennium is not a utopia but a spiritual reign.
- Christ is seated, reigning, and ruling from heaven.
- His saints are part of this kingdom now, through faith and the new birth.
- The apostles and early Christians believed this and staked their lives on it.

The millennium is not something we wait for—it is something we live in.

We are kingdom people, awaiting the King's return—not to *begin* his reign but to *bring it to full visibility*.

It's a fair and important question: *If Satan is bound now, why does so much evil still exist in the world?* But the truth is, *no serious theological view—amillennial or otherwise—claims that evil is absent today*. What amillennialism affirms is that Satan's influence has been *strategically restrained* so that the gospel might go forth freely to the nations during this present age.

We do not deny the presence of sin, suffering, or spiritual warfare. What we affirm is that *Christ reigns in the midst of it*, and his kingdom is advancing in ways that Satan can no longer stop. But we also know this isn't the end of the story.

Amillennialism holds that the reign of Christ continues *until he returns*—and when he does, *evil will finally and forever be destroyed*. Satan will be released for one final act of rebellion, but his defeat is certain. That is where we turn next:

What happens at the end—and after—the millennium?

Chapter 4

What Comes Next?

IN THE PREVIOUS CHAPTER, we explored the present reality of the millennium—a reign of Christ that is already underway. The thousand years mentioned in Rev 20 is not a future era waiting to begin but a current spiritual reality in which Christ rules through his church.

Yet this reign will not last forever. The Bible is clear that this present age, this millennium, will one day come to a dramatic conclusion. But it's not just important to know that the millennium ends—it's crucial to understand how it ends.

Interestingly, both traditional amillennialists and premillennialists agree on this point: the millennium ends violently. It culminates with Satan being released from his prison, going on a final rampage to deceive the nations and rally a last rebellion against God's people. Though they differ on the timing and nature of the millennium itself, these two major perspectives converge here.

What follows this tumultuous period, however, is a phase that all believers look forward to with eager anticipation. It is a time of final judgment, the ultimate defeat of evil, and the ushering in of God's new creation—a new heaven and a new earth where righteousness dwells and God's people live with him forever.

As we enter this chapter, our goal is to understand this critical "end of the end." What does Scripture teach about the brief resurgence of evil after the millennium? How is this rebellion defeated? And what awaits God's people after this final confrontation?

By exploring these questions carefully, we gain not only theological clarity but practical hope—hope that in the face of evil and deception, God's victory is sure, and the best is yet to come.

The "Little While"—What Is It? (Revelation 20:7-8)

The phrase "for a little while" appears in Rev 20:7, where John writes, "And when the thousand years are ended, Satan will be released from his prison and will come out to deceive the nations that are at the four corners of the earth." The Greek phrase *mikron chronon*, translated "a little while," is a fascinating phrase packed with significance.

What does this "little while" mean? Is it a brief moment? A short but intense period? Or simply a symbolic phrase?

Traditional Interpretations

Both traditional amillennial and premillennial interpreters recognize this "little while" as a short period following the millennium—but they understand it differently.

Premillennialists often take this as a literal future event where Satan is released after a thousand-year earthly reign of Christ. They see this release as a visible, physical event just before the final judgment, marking the last desperate rebellion against Christ's kingdom.

Traditional amillennialists, on the other hand, understand the "little while" as a symbolic yet real interval of intensified evil. This period is not some far-off physical reign of Christ on earth but a short, severe time of spiritual opposition and persecution just before Christ's return.

A Future Visible Resurgence of Evil

My perspective aligns broadly with the traditional amillennial understanding that this "little while" represents a future, though brief, outpouring of satanic deception and rebellion before the final consummation. Yet it's important to recognize this is not merely symbolic or abstract.

The "little while" should be taken seriously as a visible resurgence of evil—a time when Satan's influence will swell and persecutions may intensify. It may last a generation or less, but it will be intense and unmistakable.

This "little while" aligns closely with several other biblical passages describing a future time of intense tribulation and deception shortly before Christ's return.

In the book of Daniel, we read about a period of "time, times, and half a time" (Dan 7:25; 12:7), often understood as three and a half years—half of a symbolic seven-year period. This time is marked by persecution of God's people and attempts to change times and laws, a vivid portrayal of opposition to God's kingdom.

Jesus, in his Olivet discourse recorded in Matt 24, Mark 13, and Luke 21, warns his disciples about a future tribulation unlike anything the world has seen before. He says in Matt 24:21, "For then there will be great tribulation, such as has not been from the beginning of the world until now, no, and never will be." This tribulation involves false messiahs, widespread persecution, cosmic signs, and great distress.

Revelation also depicts this period through various judgments and woes, often focused around the seven-year tribulation framework divided into two halves of three-and-a-half years each (Rev 11:2–3; 12:6, 14; 13:5).

From this perspective, the "little while" after the millennium is the final, fierce outpouring of satanic deception and rebellion. Though brief in comparison to the millennial reign, it is a concentrated period of intense spiritual warfare, cultural apostasy, and persecution.

Why Would This Period Be So Terrible?

What makes this "little while" of rebellion so devastating? One undeniable factor is Satan himself being released from his prison. After being restrained for the millennium, he is freed to deceive the nations once again. But there may be another significant event happening alongside this: the rapture of the church.

The "secret rapture" of the church refers to the belief that Christ will come unexpectedly and invisibly to remove believers from the earth before a future period of tribulation and judgment. This view, commonly called the *pre-tribulation rapture*, teaches that the church will be caught up ("raptured") to meet Christ in the air prior to his visible second coming. Most scholars agree that this specific doctrine is a relatively new development in church history, first articulated by John Nelson Darby in the 1830s and popularized through the *Scofield Reference Bible*. However, being a new doctrine does not necessarily make it wrong. Christian theology has often developed over time as believers studied Scripture more deeply—such as with the formation of the Trinity or the clarification of justification by faith. The critical issue, therefore, is not whether there will be a rapture—since 1 Thess 4:16–17 affirms that believers will be caught up with Christ—but rather *when* it will occur in relation to the tribulation and Christ's final return. The debate centers on timing and interpretation, not on the reality of Christ's ultimate gathering of his people.

Imagine for a moment the impact if Satan's release and the rapture occur in unison. The sudden removal of millions of believers—the restraining presence of the Spirit-empowered church on earth—would create a vacuum of spiritual resistance. Without the faithful witnesses and the Holy Spirit's convicting power visibly working through the church, deception and lawlessness would multiply rapidly.

Jesus promised his followers that after his ascension, he would send the Holy Spirit to empower them for witness and perseverance (Acts 1:8). Paul also speaks of a "restrainer" being removed before the day of the Lord comes (2 Thess 2:6–7). While the identity of the restrainer is debated, many understand it to be the Spirit's work through the church.

If God sends his Spirit, it is only fitting that he could also remove the restrainer—removing the church's influence by rapturing believers to heaven. This divine removal would allow Satan greater freedom to work unchecked.

Together, Satan's release and the removal of the restraining church would unleash unparalleled spiritual deception and persecution. It would be a time of darkness and lawlessness unlike anything history has ever witnessed—a global rebellion fueled by lies and hatred against God's kingdom.

This combination explains why Jesus warns of a tribulation so severe it surpasses all others (Matt 24:21). It also underscores the urgency for the church to stand firm, remain vigilant, and cling to Christ amid increasing trials.

Israel's Role in the Final Rebellion

Though I affirm an amillennial understanding of the millennium as Christ's present spiritual reign, I also recognize the biblical importance of Israel and the Middle East in the end-times drama. For the final rebellion described in Revelation and Daniel to unfold as Scripture portrays, certain key events likely must occur in that region—most notably, the building of a new temple in Jerusalem.

The prophecy of a "desolating sacrilege" or desecration (Dan 9:27; Matt 24:15) implies that a temple will be in place to be defiled. This means that at some point, a new temple—whether literal or symbolic—would be established before the "little while" of rebellion.

Therefore, while the millennium is primarily a spiritual reality, the physical nation of Israel and events in the Middle East remain critical signs to watch. The rise of conflict, the temple's establishment, and the ensuing desecration may mark the onset of this intense final tribulation.

Keeping an eye on these developments does not contradict Amillennialism but rather reflects a balanced attentiveness to biblical prophecy and contemporary history.

Integrating the Time Frames

By linking Rev 20:7's "little while" with Daniel's "time, times, and half a time" and Jesus' Olivet discourse, we can understand this final rebellion as the culmination of God's redemptive timeline—a brief but severe period of tribulation that tests the faithfulness of God's people.

This means that even though Christ currently reigns spiritually, there remains a divine allowance for this short season of evil to fully expose the rebellious hearts of humanity before the final and decisive intervention of Christ at his return.

Real-World Parallels: History and Warning

History provides sobering examples of such times. Consider the rise of totalitarian regimes that aggressively suppress the gospel and Christian witness—Nazi Germany's brutal persecution, North Korea's ongoing religious oppression, or even contemporary global trends of hostility toward biblical Christianity.

These are glimpses of what the "little while" could look like on a global scale. The gospel may be pushed underground; believers may face imprisonment, violence, or exile; and cultural hostility may reach unprecedented levels.

This is not a call to despair but a sober warning—and a call to readiness. The church must stand firm, confident in Christ's ultimate victory even when evil appears to surge.

Theological Significance

Theologically, this "little while" underscores that Christ's reign, though currently victorious, allows a limited window for rebellion to surface. Satan's binding during the millennium is not permanent until this final phase.

This temporary release serves a divine purpose: to reveal the depths of human depravity and the futility of rebellion without God. It also vindicates God's righteous judgment and the justice of the final condemnation.

Gog and Magog—Global Rebellion, Not Geographic

> To gather them for battle; their number is like the sand of the sea. (Rev 20:8)

Immediately following Satan's release during the "little while," John describes a global uprising symbolized by the names Gog and Magog. These two names, pulled from the prophetic literature of Ezek 38–39, have long stirred debate. Are they literal nations? Future alliances? Or symbolic representations?

The answer, I believe, is both clearer and more sobering than most popular speculation allows.

The Background in Ezekiel

To understand John's use of Gog and Magog, we must revisit their origin in Ezekiel's vision. In Ezek 38–39, Gog is portrayed as a prince from the land of Magog, leading a massive coalition of nations from the north to attack God's people. The intent is total annihilation, but God intervenes decisively, raining fire and judgment upon the invaders. The result is unmistakable: God's sovereignty and glory are revealed to the nations, and his people are delivered.

This prophecy, like much of Ezekiel's writing, is rich in apocalyptic imagery. While the nations mentioned had some historical grounding, many scholars—especially those in the amillennial tradition—understand Ezekiel's vision as a symbolic portrayal of the final opposition to God's rule, not a literal, geographically defined battle.

John picks up on this imagery in Rev 20 but expands it. He no longer speaks of Gog as a northern ruler over a small coalition. Instead, Gog and Magog now represent "the nations that are at the four corners of the earth." This is a key interpretive shift. What was once local and limited in Ezekiel becomes global and universal in Revelation.

Not a War in the Middle East

Many premillennial interpreters expect a literal war in or around Israel, with Russia, Iran, or some modern equivalent fulfilling the role of Gog. But within the amillennial framework—and in my own view—this misses the point of John's symbolic use of the names. Gog and Magog are not about geography; they are about global rebellion.

This is not about tanks in the Golan Heights or drones over Jerusalem. It's about the spirit of antichrist uniting the world in hatred and opposition to Christ and his people. It's not just a military assault but a cultural, ideological, and spiritual uprising. A total revolt against the lordship of Christ.

A Unified World Against Christ

This is where I believe our modern world gives us a glimpse of what's possible. For the first time in history, the nations of the world are truly connected—politically, economically, digitally, and culturally. The tools for unifying global rebellion already exist.

Imagine a world system that turns against biblical Christianity with legislative, technological, and military power—a world where Christians are labeled as threats to peace or progress—a time where truth is suppressed, and deception is mass produced.

From media to marketplaces, education to entertainment, there could come a time where hostility toward Christ is not regional but universal. This is the rebellion of Gog and Magog—not a single invasion but a worldwide movement fueled by satanic deception and human pride.

Traditional Amillennial View vs. Expanded Insight

Traditional amillennialists rightly see Gog and Magog as symbolic of the final surge of opposition to Christ before his return. I affirm this view but want to expand it to account for the unique conditions of our time. Modern technology, social cohesion, and global ideology could all be tools in Satan's hand during this final surge. This would not be a battle with tanks and troops but with propaganda, surveillance, persecution, and spiritual darkness.

Gog and Magog symbolize not geography but globality. Not a place but a posture. Not a momentary skirmish but a final, coordinated uprising of fallen humanity under Satan's brief resurgence.

Fire from Heaven—No Final Battle?

> But fire came down from heaven and consumed them. (Rev 20:9)

After describing the global rebellion of Gog and Magog, John gives us a startlingly abrupt ending to the uprising. There is no prolonged war, no clash of armies, no drawn-out struggle. Instead, we're told simply, "But fire came down from heaven and consumed them."

That's it.

This is a hallmark of the amillennial interpretation—what appears to be the buildup to a global war ends with divine intervention, not military conflict. There is no Armageddon in the traditional cinematic sense. The final rebellion is over before it truly begins. Christ doesn't need to negotiate or mobilize troops. He ends the rebellion with fire from heaven—instant, unmistakable judgment.

This echoes the language of 2 Thess 2:8: "Then the lawless one will be revealed, whom the Lord Jesus will kill with the breath of his mouth and bring to nothing by the appearance of his coming."

The same God who created with a word can destroy with a word. Christ's return is not the beginning of a battle; it is the end of one. His very presence is enough to obliterate opposition.

Eyes of Fire, Fire from Heaven: A Theological Connection

Revelation 19:12 describes Jesus at his triumphant return, saying,

> His eyes were like a flame of fire.

Then, in Rev 20:9, as the nations gather against the camp of the saints, we read,

> But fire came down from heaven and consumed them.

At first glance, these may seem like disconnected images—one is descriptive, the other is destructive. However, when viewed through the lens of *Christ's active reign* and *symbolic judgment*, a compelling theological connection emerges.

Christ's Eyes of Fire: Symbol of Penetrating Judgment

The image of *eyes like fire* in Rev 19 (also seen in Rev 1:14 and 2:18) points to Jesus' *omniscient discernment, holy indignation*, and *purifying judgment*. Fire here is not literal but spiritual—his gaze sees through falsehood, hypocrisy, and rebellion. It is a *consuming righteousness* that cannot be evaded or deceived.

This fire is not passive. It symbolizes a *living, active, divine energy*—Jesus doesn't just come to judge; he *is* the judge. His presence brings either *refining fire for the redeemed or devouring fire for the wicked*.

Fire from Heaven: The Same Judgment Manifested

In Rev 20:9, when Satan deceives the nations for "a little while," they gather to wage war against "the camp of the saints." But the conflict ends before it starts:

> Fire came down from heaven and consumed them.

This "fire from heaven" is not the result of a cosmic missile strike—it is a symbol of *divine, final judgment*. Just as God judged Sodom with fire (Gen 19) or consumed Nadab and Abihu (Lev 10), here, too, fire represents *God's immediate and righteous wrath*.

And who is the agent of that wrath?

According to Rev 19, it is *Christ himself*, riding in victory. The *eyes of fire* in 19:12 are now *fire from heaven* in 20:9. It is the same divine judgment—first described *in Christ's nature*, now enacted *in Christ's authority*.

Theological Bridge: Christ Is the Fire

In both images,

- the source is heaven
- the fire is judgment
- the object is evil and rebellion

Rather than seeing Rev 20 as a separate chronological event, amillennial theology sees these as *recapitulations*—different symbolic angles on the same truth.

Christ has conquered. He sees. He judges. He reigns.

Thus, Rev 19–20 is not about two events but *one reality revealed in two powerful metaphors*:

- In Rev 19, *he comes as the Judge.*
- In Rev 20, *he executes final judgment.*

Both are fire. Both are holy. Both are Christ.

Application: A Fire That Comforts and Confronts

To the believer, his fire is a *purifying grace*. To the rebel, it is a *consuming wrath*.

This theological connection gives Revelation's apocalyptic imagery a deep pastoral edge. Christ's gaze is searching, not just in the future but *now*. His fire burns away idols, lies, and facades. It exposes and cleanses. And in the end, that same fire will make all things right.

How It Fits the Amillennial View

Rather than teaching two separate second comings or millennia, amillennialism sees the fire of chapter 19 and the fire of chapter 20 as *literary echoes*—not chronological steps.

The visions in Revelation are not sequential blueprints but *symbolic overlays of one redemptive climax*—the victory of Christ.

Could There Still Be a Final Battle?

Yet, while the text offers this sudden ending, it doesn't necessarily rule out the possibility of a final battle attempt—a confrontation that starts but doesn't last. From a prophetic perspective, there may be physical or ideological mobilization, even a global campaign launched against God's people. Perhaps governments, militaries, or coalitions align to destroy the church or Israel or both.

But even if such a final battle is initiated, it ends before it can accomplish anything. It is crushed, not by earthly resistance but by heavenly fire. In other words, the outcome is never in question. Whether it is a war that fizzles out in divine fire or a rebellion cut short in planning stages, the truth remains: Christ and his saints win.

Victory Belongs to the Lamb

Whether symbolic or real, ideological or physical, the final rebellion leads not to panic but to praise. The enemy gathers, the world rages, the church endures—and then, in one glorious moment, the skies break open, and the King returns.

This is the hope of every believer. Not that we escape all trials or avoid all tribulation, but that in the end, we are on the winning side. The fire from heaven reminds us that evil has a deadline. Rebellion has a reckoning. And Christ has no rival.

The Great White Throne Judgment

> Then I saw a great white throne and him who was seated on it. From his presence earth and sky fled away, and no place was found for them. (Rev 20:11)

Immediately following the defeat of Gog and Magog, John turns our attention to one of the most sobering and awe-inspiring scenes in all of Scripture—the great white throne judgment. The imagery is unmistakable: a majestic throne, a divine judge, and all humanity standing before him.

This is not symbolic. This is real, final, and inescapable. The end of the millennium leads directly into this final moment of cosmic accountability.

Judgment Before the King

John describes the dead, "great and small," standing before the throne. No one is exempt. This is the resurrection of all people—the righteous and the unrighteous—now standing before the Judge of all the earth.

Jesus foretold this moment in John 5:28–29:

> Do not marvel at this, for an hour is coming when all who are in the tombs will hear his voice and come out, those

who have done good to the resurrection of life, and those who have done evil to the resurrection of judgment.

This is what theologians refer to as the general resurrection, not two separate events divided by a thousand years but one climactic moment where all are raised and judged. The amillennial view holds that the resurrection, judgment, and return of Christ all occur together in a single, comprehensive event.

I affirm this view—and would add that this unified sequence helps us make better sense of the flow of Rev 20. The order is logical and consistent:

- the "little while" of rebellion (vv. 7–9)
- the crushing of Satan's uprising (v. 9)
- the final judgment (vv. 11–15)
- the new heavens and new earth (Rev 21)

No need for complex gaps, timelines, or separated judgments—just the unrolling of God's final plan in swift and sovereign order.

The Books Are Opened

John says that "books were opened," including another book, the book of life. These books represent both divine record and divine grace. Every deed, thought, and motive is accounted for. Justice will be done, perfectly and without error.

But the book of life reminds us that salvation is not based on deeds alone. Those who belong to Christ—whose names are written in the Lamb's book of life—are spared from the second death. Their judgment is not condemnation but vindication.

This echoes Paul's words in Rom 8:1:

> There is therefore now no condemnation for those who are in Christ Jesus.

For the unbelieving world, this moment will be one of holy terror. But for those in Christ, it is not a day of dread—it is a day of deliverance. The Judge is also our Savior.

A Clear and Final Division

The outcome of this judgment is final and irreversible. Revelation 20:15 says,

> If anyone's name was not found written in the book of life, he was thrown into the lake of fire.

This is what Scripture calls the second death—eternal separation from God, final judgment on sin, and the end of all rebellion. But for believers, this moment ushers in the fullness of life in God's presence. As Jesus said in Matt 25:34, the King will say,

> Come, you who are blessed by my Father, inherit the kingdom prepared for you from the foundation of the world.

A Moment That Demands Preparation

This judgment scene isn't just theological—it's deeply personal. Everyone will be there. Every life will be evaluated. Every name will either be found in the book of life or not.

For the unbelieving world, this moment will be one of holy terror. But for those in Christ, the tone is different. Scripture is clear: "There is therefore now no condemnation for those who are in Christ Jesus" (Rom 8:1).

This promise remains unshaken—even in the face of judgment. If you are in Christ, you will not be condemned. The second death holds no power over you (see Rev 20:6).

Yet, that does not mean believers are exempt from judgment altogether. The Bible consistently teaches that we will still stand before Christ and give an account—not to determine salvation but to reveal faithfulness and receive reward.

Paul writes in 2 Cor 5:10, "For we must all appear before the judgment seat of Christ, so that each one may receive what is due for what he has done in the body, whether good or evil."

Likewise, in Rom 14:10–12, Paul says, "For we will all stand before the judgment seat of God. . . . So then each of us will give an account of himself to God."

This is likely the moment Jesus referred to when he spoke of storing up "treasures in heaven" (Matt 6:19–21). The rewards believers receive at this judgment may correspond to their faithfulness, sacrifice, and stewardship during their lives on earth. This is the time when the crowns mentioned throughout the New Testament—such as the crown of life (Jas 1:12), the crown of righteousness (2 Tim 4:8), and the imperishable crown (1 Cor 9:25)—are given.

None of these rewards will be based on merit in a salvific sense. Salvation is by grace alone. But God, in his generosity, still honors faithful service. As Jesus said in Matt 25:21, "Well done, good and faithful servant. . . . Enter into the joy of your master."

This understanding brings urgency—but also hope. We are not judged for our sins—that debt was paid in full at the cross—but we are judged for what we've done with the grace we've been given.

The Second Death and the End of Satan

> And the devil who had deceived them was thrown into the lake of fire and sulfur where the beast and the false prophet were, and they will be tormented day and night forever and ever. (Rev 20:10)

With the final rebellion crushed and judgment rendered, Scripture turns its attention to the final fate of Satan himself. The deceiver, who has been active from the garden of Eden to the end of the millennium, now meets his eternal end.

There is no further conflict, no second chance, and no future escape. Satan is cast into the lake of fire—permanently.

This moment is not symbolic. It is definitive, conclusive, and eternal. The enemy of God and man is finally and forever defeated.

The Completion of the Cycle

This fulfills the narrative arc that began in Rev 20:1, where Satan was bound for a thousand years. That binding limited his ability to deceive the nations and restrained him during the church age. His release for a "little while" allowed for one final demonstration of human rebellion and spiritual warfare.

But now the cycle is complete:

- Satan is bound (Rev 20:2–3).
- Satan is released (Rev 20:7).
- Satan is destroyed (Rev 20:10).

The deceiver is not rehabilitated or re-imprisoned. He is cast into the lake of fire, where he will be tormented day and night forever and ever. There is no parole, no future rebellion, no escape from this judgment. Evil, in its most personal form, is eradicated forever.

This moment echoes Jesus' teaching in Matt 25:41, where he speaks of the eternal fire "prepared for the devil and his angels." Hell is not a metaphor—it is the ultimate justice of God poured out on unrepentant evil. And Satan is its first and foremost inhabitant.

The Second Death: Final Separation

Alongside Satan's judgment, Rev 20:14–15 also speaks of the "second death"—the lake of fire—as the final destiny of all whose names are not found in the book of life. The second death is not annihilation but eternal conscious separation from God. It is a place of unending judgment and regret.

Jesus spoke plainly about this in Matt 10:28:

Rather fear him who can destroy both soul and body in hell.

Paul describes it as "eternal destruction, away from the presence of the Lord and from the glory of his might" (2 Thess 1:9).

The second death is a terrifying reality—and a necessary one. It demonstrates that God is not indifferent to evil. He will not allow rebellion to go unchecked. The holiness of God demands justice, and in the end, that justice is perfectly served.

For the Believer: Assurance, Not Fear

For those in Christ, the second death holds no threat. Revelation 20:6 offers this promise: "Blessed and holy is the one who shares in the first resurrection! Over such the second death has no power."

Believers are not only spared from judgment—they are given life. Eternal life. Life in God's presence. Life without sin, Satan, or sorrow.

This section reminds us that Satan is not just bound—he is doomed. Evil is not just restrained—it is obliterated. For all the chaos and deception he's sown throughout history, Satan's end is total and final.

And that end is not a tragedy—it's a triumph. The King has won. The Judge has ruled. The serpent's head is crushed forever.

I hope you are beginning to see that there are more similarities than previously thought between premillennial and amillennial views on the end of days. While amillennialism is not chart-friendly, the following chart shows traditional views and a modified "dispensational amillennial view."

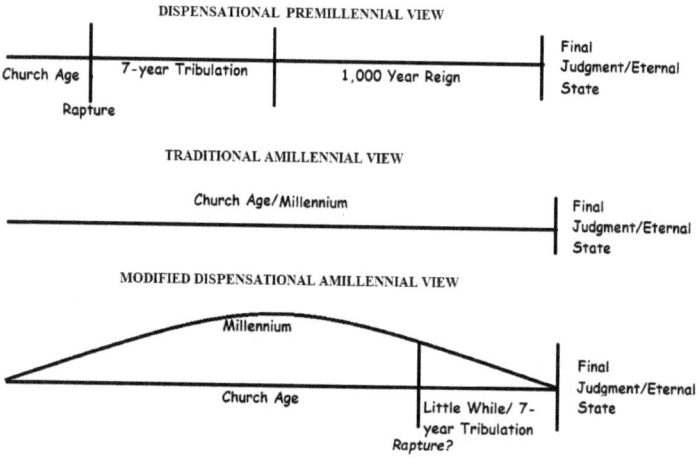

In my view, we are in both the church age *and* millennium reign of Christ. It's biblical that Christ is seated on the throne at the right hand of the father. The gospel is spreading throughout the nations because Satan is bound. Unfortunately, there is coming a time where he will be released. While Revelation only says it's for a "little while," I believe this directly correlates to the seven-year great tribulation. I believe it is highly likely that the church will be removed, "raptured" before this occurs, but even if not, this little while is just that.

After this little while comes the final judgment and Satan will be destroyed forever and ever. There will be a new heaven and new earth, and the elect will live happily ever after.

Why This Matters for Today

The study of eschatology—of things to come—is not meant to fill our heads with speculation but to fuel our hearts with hope and perseverance. Revelation 20 is not simply a mysterious apocalyptic chapter tucked into the end of the Bible. It's a clear reminder that history is going somewhere and that God is sovereign over every moment, even the chaos to come.

Evil Is Real—but It's Also Temporary

We live in a world filled with deception, persecution, confusion, and compromise. Evil seems to be gaining ground in culture, politics, education, and even inside some churches. But we must not forget the promise embedded in this chapter: Satan's days are numbered. His final rebellion is not a sign of victory but desperation. He is released "for a little while"—a brief season before his eternal defeat.

This means that, though we feel the pressure of the times, the end of evil is guaranteed. It is not indefinite. It will not spiral beyond God's reach. Satan may roar, but he cannot reign.

The Church Must Be Watchful and Faithful

Because this final season could be marked by mass deception, apostasy, and persecution, believers must not be passive. We are not promised ease but endurance. Jesus warned of a tribulation unlike anything before (Matt 24:21). Paul told the Thessalonians to stay alert because a "man of lawlessness" would come before the day of the Lord (2 Thess 2:3-4). And Rev 20 reminds us that even at the end, evil does not go quietly.

This is not cause for panic—but preparation. We know who wins. But we must endure faithfully until the end (Matt 24:13). As Jesus said, "In this world you will have trouble. But take heart! I have overcome the world" (John 16:33).

We Will All Stand Before Christ

Every one of us will stand before the throne. For the believer, there is no condemnation (Rom 8:1)—but there will be evaluation. Our works will be tested (1 Cor 3:13-15), and Jesus promised to reward faithfulness (Matt 25:21; Rev 22:12). This is likely where we receive the "treasures in heaven" (Matt 6:20) and the "crown of righteousness" (2 Tim 4:8).

For the unbeliever, this is the moment of final judgment. The second death awaits those whose names are not in the book of life. This sobering truth should move us to urgency in our witness and compassion in our evangelism.

Hope on the Horizon

So why does this matter today?

Because soon and very soon, Christ will return—and Satan will be done forever.

Every tear will be wiped away. Every injustice will be corrected. Every wrong will be undone. We are not moving toward chaos but toward consummation.

The millennium ends.
The rebellion is crushed.
The judgment is righteous.
The devil is done.
The church is triumphant.
And eternity begins.

This is the story we are a part of. This is the hope we hold onto. This is why we press on.

> He who testifies to these things says, "Surely I am coming soon." Amen. Come, Lord Jesus! (Rev 22:20)

Chapter 5

Israel and the End of Days
God's Plan, Our Posture

Why Israel Still Matters

SAY THE WORD "ISRAEL" in an eschatology discussion and you'll often watch a room divide. Some see a modern miracle and prophetic fulfillment in the rebirth of the nation in 1948. Others see a political entity with theological baggage. But if we're going to approach eschatology seriously—and biblically—we cannot ignore Israel. To do so would be to overlook one of the clearest threads running through both testaments: God's covenant faithfulness to his people.

Covenant Still Stands

Israel matters because God said so. His promise to Abraham in Gen 12—that through his seed all nations would be blessed—is reiterated to Isaac, Jacob, and expanded through the Law and the Prophets. While many of those promises were fulfilled in Christ (Gal 3:16), the nation of Israel still holds significance in redemptive history. Paul, writing in Rom 11, makes it plain: "As regards election, they are beloved for the sake of their forefathers. For the gifts and the calling of God are irrevocable" (vv. 28–29).

This does not mean that modern political Israel automatically equals covenantal Israel. But it does mean that God has not forgotten his ancient people. Amillennialism rightly emphasizes the continuity between Old Testament Israel and the New Testament church, but that does not erase the unique role of ethnic Israel in God's grand design. If we're not careful, we can fall into either of two ditches: treating Israel as a prophetic stopwatch or dismissing her entirely as irrelevant.

The 1948 Tension

For many, the founding of the modern state of Israel in 1948 was nothing short of prophetic. For dispensationalists, it was a major eschatological marker, a sign that the end times clock had begun ticking again after centuries of pause. Israel was back in the land. Surely the rapture must be around the corner.

This view understandably carries emotional and spiritual weight. The Holocaust had just devastated the Jewish people. The idea that prophecy was being fulfilled in real time electrified pulpits and prophecy conferences across the West. It also solidified dispensationalism's hold on American evangelicalism.

This is also where many reject amillennialism. "If Israel is in the land again," they argue, "how can you say there's no future for Israel? Doesn't this prove that God's plan for the nation is ongoing?" And to their credit, it's a fair question. But we must be careful not to confuse historical events with biblical fulfillment unless Scripture plainly tells us to.

Amillennialism does not deny that Israel matters. It simply argues that the people of God—now including both Jews and gentiles united in Christ—are the true fulfillment of the Abrahamic promises. That doesn't erase national Israel from history, but it places her role within the larger redemptive story rather than at the prophetic center.

Israel and the End of Days

Bridging the Divide

Here's where it gets interesting: amillennialists and dispensationalists may disagree on timelines, the millennium, and the nature of prophetic fulfillment—but both views affirm that God has a purpose for Israel. Where they differ is in what that purpose looks like.

Amillennialism doesn't reject the possibility of a future turning of ethnic Israel to Christ. Romans 11:26 says, "And in this way all Israel will be saved," a passage that allows for multiple interpretations but none that completely exclude the Jewish people. Many amillennialists believe this refers to a final ingathering of Jewish people into the faith before Christ's return—a vision not altogether different from some dispensational hopes, albeit without the accompanying geopolitical program.

So, let's say it clearly: the rebirth of Israel in 1948 is historically significant. It may even be providential. But it is not, in and of itself, proof of a dispensational timeline. Nor is it a reason to reject amillennialism. A faithful amillennial view can still make space for God's future work among ethnic Jews, rooted not in political Israel's survival but in the gospel's power to save to the uttermost.

We don't have to throw out every prophetic insight from our dispensational brothers, nor do we need to ignore the theological richness of covenantal continuity. The two can—and sometimes should—be in conversation. Where we must draw the line is allowing geopolitical events to dictate our doctrine rather than letting Scripture do so.

Israel in Biblical Prophecy

From the first whispers of redemption in Genesis to the fiery apocalyptic visions of Revelation, Israel is in the story. She is both stage and player in God's drama of salvation. So when we ask, "Does Israel have a role in biblical prophecy?" the answer is yes—but the "how" depends heavily on your eschatological lens.

Let's take a closer look at what the Bible actually says—and what it doesn't.

A Story Still Unfolding

The Old Testament prophets consistently spoke of a time when God would restore his people. Passages like Ezek 36–37, Amos 9:11–15, and Zech 12–14 anticipate a renewal of Israel—both in land and in heart. These are powerful texts, full of vivid imagery and covenantal language: dry bones rising, ruined cities rebuilt, a fountain opened for sin and uncleanness.

The question becomes: when and how are these prophecies fulfilled?

Dispensationalists generally hold that many of these promises are yet future and will be literally fulfilled in a millennial kingdom, with national Israel restored geographically and spiritually after the second coming of Christ. For them, these texts point to a thousand-year reign on earth, headquartered in Jerusalem, with Jesus ruling visibly over a Jewish-led kingdom.

Amillennialists, by contrast, argue that these texts find their fulfillment in Christ's first coming, the outpouring of the Spirit at Pentecost, and the global expansion of the church. They read Ezekiel's valley of dry bones as a metaphor for spiritual rebirth in Christ. They see the rebuilt tent of David in Amos 9 as the church gathered from every nation (Acts 15:14–18 confirms this interpretation). In this view, Israel's prophetic hope is not delayed—it has already begun.

Yet even the most covenantal amillennialist cannot ignore that Paul devotes three full chapters in Romans (9–11) to the question of Israel's future. He affirms that "not all who are descended from Israel belong to Israel" (Rom 9:6), but he also holds out hope for a future turning of the Jewish people to Christ.

The takeaway? Both views are trying to honor the biblical text. One emphasizes future fulfillment in national and geographic terms. The other emphasizes present fulfillment in spiritual and global terms. Neither denies God's love for Israel. The debate is over how that love is expressed and fulfilled in redemptive history.

Prophetic Warnings and Invitations

Joel 3, Zech 14, and Revelation all mention climactic battles and gatherings in or around Jerusalem. This is another sticking point in eschatological debates. Some insist these are literal events yet to come. Others interpret them symbolically, as depicting the final conflict between the kingdom of God and the forces of evil.

So how do we handle texts that describe nations gathering against Israel?

We must read prophecy with humility. Much of it is poetic, apocalyptic, or symbolic in nature. Even when the language is vivid and geographic, its ultimate aim is spiritual. For example, the "Mount Zion" of Isa 2:2 is later interpreted in Heb 12:22 as a reference to the heavenly Jerusalem, not merely a hill outside the city walls.

Still, there's no denying that Jerusalem is often the setting of prophetic drama. God chose that city for a reason. It was the place where his name would dwell. It was where Jesus was crucified and resurrected. And it may well be the city where the final curtain falls. But whether literal or symbolic, the point remains: God will vindicate his people and judge the nations who oppose him.

The key is not to obsess over topography but to understand the theological purpose: God keeps his word. God protects his people. God judges wickedness and rewards faithfulness. These are truths all eschatological views can affirm.

Modern Israel ≠ Ancient Covenant

One crucial distinction must be made: the modern political state of Israel is not the same thing as biblical Israel under covenant. This is a mistake made on both sides of the debate.

- Some dispensationalists treat the current nation as a direct fulfillment of Old Testament promises.
- Some amillennialists swing too far in the other direction, ignoring Israel altogether.

The truth is somewhere in between. Modern Israel may be part of God's providence, but it is not above critique, nor is it the church's replacement. Christians must view Israel with both biblical compassion and theological clarity.

In the prophetic timeline, Israel matters not merely because of her geography or politics but because of her role in the story of redemption. She is a signpost that still points us to God's covenant faithfulness and sovereign purposes—even if we disagree on how those purposes unfold.

What Should We Be Watching For?

Jesus' words in Matt 24 ring with urgency: "Watch therefore, for you do not know what hour your Lord is coming." Every generation of believers has been called to watch—not with sensationalism or speculative charts but with eyes of faith and hearts anchored in truth.

But what does watching look like, especially when it comes to Israel and the end of days?

If we truly believe that God is not finished with Israel—and that history is moving toward a divinely appointed climax—then the people of God must remain spiritually alert and discerning. Jesus often commanded his followers to "watch and pray." The apostle Paul reminded believers that "we are not of the night or of darkness . . . so then let us not sleep, as others do, but let us keep awake and be sober" (1 Thess 5:5–6).

So what should we be watching for in the unfolding days ahead?

Christ Preparing His Bride

While much prophetic speculation often centers on world events, wars, or the latest developments in the Middle East, we must not lose sight of the quiet but powerful work of Christ sanctifying his church. Ephesians 5:27 says he is purifying a people for himself, "without spot or wrinkle . . . holy and without blemish." This is not abstract theology—it's a call for readiness.

Rather than looking exclusively at geopolitical signs, we should see every revival, every missionary breakthrough, and every move of the Spirit as part of the bride's preparation. The church will not limp into glory. Christ will present her in splendor. The question we must ask is not just, "What is happening in Israel?" but, "What is happening in us?"

A Third Temple: The Final Deception?

This is where discernment is key. While the rebuilding of a third temple in Jerusalem would be hailed by many as the pinnacle of prophetic fulfillment, it may in fact serve as a strategic tool in the final deception.

From my perspective—and in harmony with the "little while" discussed in chapter 4—I do expect a third temple to be rebuilt during that brief time of Satan's release. But it won't usher in Christ's reign. Instead, it may very well serve as a counterfeit fulfillment that unifies the world in false worship. Revelation speaks of the "man of lawlessness" (2 Thess 2:3–4), the "abomination of desolation" (Matt 24:15), and a global system of deceit energized by Satan himself. The temple could become a focal point in this deception—a religious symbol used to mask rebellion against God.

We should not dismiss the third temple lightly, nor should we celebrate it uncritically. Its construction may indeed be prophetic, but not as a sign of hope. It may be the final stage before the fire falls.

Revelation 20:9 says, "Fire came down from heaven and consumed them," echoing the fiery eyes of Christ in Rev 19:12. The same Jesus who sees all and judges righteously will bring an end to the deception. This temple, built in the name of peace or prophecy, will be halted by the King of kings. That moment will not mark a new age of earthly rule but the end of the age altogether.

The Convergence of Global Systems

One of the most compelling signs to watch for is the increasing convergence of global systems—economic, political, technological, and religious. Revelation 13 portrays a scenario where "no one can buy or sell unless he has the mark" and where worship of the beast becomes universal. While the exact interpretation of the "mark" varies across eschatological frameworks, most agree it points to a time of unprecedented control and conformity under a global authority.

Today, we are witnessing the rapid acceleration of global connectivity. Digital currencies, artificial intelligence, surveillance technologies, and even biometric identification systems are becoming normalized. While these tools are not evil in themselves, they offer a glimpse of how an antichrist system could be swiftly and efficiently established.

Amillennialists may interpret Revelation's imagery symbolically, seeing the beast as representing any system or government that claims divine authority and opposes Christ. Yet, even this symbolic view acknowledges the reality: there will be increasing pressure to conform to the world's values and increasing hostility toward those who remain faithful to Christ.

Consider how swiftly global mandates were adopted during the COVID-19 pandemic—travel restrictions, digital health passports, supply chain controls, and financial freezes. These mechanisms showed us how quickly the world could unite under a common system, especially when fear or crisis is involved. Again, this is not to say those events *were* the beast system but that they demonstrate its feasibility.

Christians must be prepared to live counterculturally. If we are more concerned with being accepted than being faithful, we are already vulnerable to compromise. Jesus warned in Matt 24:10 that in the last days, "many will fall away . . . and betray one another and hate one another." In that hour, the church must stand firm—not as alarmists but as anchored disciples of Jesus who know the difference between the Lamb and the beast.

The Rise of Apostasy and False Unity

Another sign Jesus and the apostles warned about repeatedly is a dramatic *falling away from the faith*. In 2 Thess 2:3, Paul says that "the rebellion" (Greek: *apostasia*) must come before the day of the Lord. Jesus warns in Matt 24:11 that "many false prophets will arise and lead many astray." This isn't merely the rise of secularism—it's *the corruption of the church from within*.

What Are We Seeing Today?

There is a growing theological and moral compromise within Christianity. Churches once grounded in Scripture are now affirming lifestyles, ideologies, and belief systems that stand in direct contradiction to God's word. The authority of Scripture is being questioned or replaced by cultural narratives.

Meanwhile, ecumenical movements are calling for interfaith unity at the expense of truth. There is a push to minimize doctrine in the name of inclusiveness—to form a kind of religious unity that sounds loving but subtly dethrones Christ as the only way to the Father.

In 2019, the Vatican and leading Islamic authorities signed the "Document on Human Fraternity," a call for religious unity and cooperation. While promoting peace is commendable, such initiatives can blur the distinctions between the true gospel and other worldviews. Many Christian leaders endorsed this agreement, stating that "God wills the diversity of religions." That claim, if taken theologically, conflicts with John 14:6 where Jesus says, "I am the way, the truth, and the life. No one comes to the Father except through me."

Amillennial Understanding

In the amillennial framework, the reign of Christ is spiritual, and the church is in constant tension with the world. This era includes wheat and tares growing side by side (Matt 13), and before the harvest, there will be a global delusion allowed by God (2 Thess 2:11). Apostasy isn't a sign that the church is failing—it's a sign that God's word is coming to pass and judgment is near.

This is not the time to "deconstruct" your faith. This is the time to reconstruct your life upon the word of God. Pastors must preach truth with clarity. Believers must hold the line, lovingly but boldly, in their families, churches, and communities. We cannot trade eternal truth for temporary peace.

Gospel Connection

False unity seeks peace without the cross. But the true unity of the church is rooted in the blood of Jesus. It's not enough to believe *in something spiritual*—salvation comes only through faith in the finished work of Christ.

The Global Persecution of the Saints

Jesus didn't just predict persecution—he promised it. In Matt 24:9, he warns, "Then they will deliver you up to tribulation and put you to death, and you will be hated by all nations for my name's sake." Similarly, Rev 13 speaks of the beast making war on the saints and conquering them. The expectation of global persecution is not a glitch in the Christian system—it's built into the end-time story.

What We Are Seeing Today

In the West, Christians are increasingly marginalized, mocked, or even labeled dangerous for holding to biblical convictions on sexuality, gender, marriage, and salvation. Laws are shifting to make Christian expression less protected. Around the world, especially in parts of Africa, the Middle East, and Asia, believers are being imprisoned, tortured, and martyred for their faith in Jesus.

This rising intolerance toward true Christianity is not random—it's prophetic. Whether through violent regimes, digital censorship, or legal pressures, the spirit of antichrist is working to silence the testimony of Jesus in the public square.

Modern Examples

In places like Nigeria and North Korea, Christians face daily threats to their lives. In the West, Christian business owners are sued for refusing to participate in events that violate their conscience. In Canada, pastors have been jailed for holding in-person worship services during COVID-19 lockdowns, while other faith groups were largely ignored. These are not isolated incidents—they are a slow, escalating trend.

Amillennial Understanding

Amillennialism teaches that Christ reigns now from heaven, even while his people suffer on earth. The "little while" described in Rev 20 involves a loosening of Satan's influence and an intensification of the war on the saints. This final storm won't destroy the church—it will refine her. The blood of the martyrs is still the seed of the church.

Dispensational Connection

While dispensationalists expect a time of tribulation after a rapture, they, too, anticipate a rise in global hostility toward Christianity beforehand. The shared recognition across views is that persecution will increase before Christ returns.

Don't be surprised when the world hates you. Be faithful. Stand firm. Be bold in your witness. Prepare your family for the cost of discipleship. Persecution is not a sign that God has abandoned us—it is a sign that his return is near and his word is true.

Gospel Connection

Jesus was falsely accused, rejected, and crucified—but he rose victorious. The persecuted church follows a crucified Savior who promises resurrection. Every lash, every loss, every imprisonment is not in vain. One day, the Lamb who was slain will return as the Lion of Judah—and justice will roll down like a mighty river.

Why This Matters for All Views

Amillennialism does not ignore Israel. It simply sees her role fulfilled in Christ and expanded through the global church. Dispensationalism may emphasize future events centered around Jerusalem, but both views agree on key essentials:

- Christ is returning bodily and visibly.
- God will judge the wicked and vindicate the righteous.
- The gospel must be proclaimed to all nations.
- God keeps his promises—even when we disagree on how.

What should we be watching for? Not just war but worship. Not just political movements but the movement of the Spirit. Not just headlines but hearts turning to Christ. These are the true signs of the times.

What We Should Be Praying For

If watching involves discernment and vigilance, praying is the believer's response in faith and intercession. The Bible calls us not only to observe the times but to act spiritually—to lift up voices on behalf of the nations, especially Israel.

Israel's Right to Exist

First, it is important to acknowledge the biblical and historical reality that Israel is God's chosen people. God declared to Abraham, "I will bless those who bless you, and him who dishonors you I will curse" (Gen 12:3). Israel's existence as a nation is not a political accident—it is part of God's sovereign plan and covenant faithfulness.

We honor their right to exist and recognize their unique place in redemptive history. As Paul affirms in Rom 11, "the gifts and the calling of God are irrevocable" (v. 29). We stand with Israel not only politically but spiritually, affirming God's enduring commitment to his people.

Yet Without Jesus, There Is No Salvation

But this acknowledgment must be paired with truth. The same God who chose Israel also demands faith in Jesus as the Messiah for salvation. Paul's heartfelt words in Rom 10:1–4 reveal his anguish and longing for Israel's salvation: "Brethren, my heart's desire and prayer to God for them is that they may be saved.... Christ is the end of the law for righteousness to everyone who believes."

Israel's national existence does not guarantee individual salvation. Without faith in Jesus, they remain under God's judgment. This is not a message of condemnation but a call to repentance and hope. The gospel is for Israel just as much as it is for the gentiles.

The Biblical Call to Pray for Israel

The Bible commands believers to pray for the peace of Jerusalem (Ps 122:6), to ask God to soften hearts (Ezek 36:26), and to intercede for Israel's spiritual awakening (Rom 11:26). Prayer is our most powerful tool in God's redemptive plan.

We should pray that

- the veil would be lifted from Jewish eyes (2 Cor 3:14).

- the promised "all Israel" will come to faith (Rom 11:26).
- God's grace and mercy would abound among the Jewish people.
- the church would be a faithful witness, loving and proclaiming the gospel boldly and humbly.

Application: Our Role in God's Plan

As believers, we have a vital role to play—not only watching but actively praying for Israel. This includes supporting ministries that reach Jewish people with the gospel, standing against anti-Semitism, and cultivating a spirit of humility and love toward God's chosen nation.

The gospel transcends politics and ethnicity. It calls all people—Jew and gentile—to bow before Christ. Let us pray earnestly and continually, knowing that God's promises will be fulfilled, and that the salvation of Israel will be a cause for great rejoicing in the kingdom.

Conclusion: Setting the Record Straight on Amillennialism and Israel

As we conclude this chapter, it is vital to set the record straight. Amillennialism is often misunderstood—and sometimes unfairly dismissed—because of its teaching on Israel and the end times. But this perspective neither minimizes Israel's significance nor ignores God's enduring promises to his chosen people.

From Genesis to Revelation, Israel remains central in God's unfolding plan of redemption. The covenants made with Abraham, Isaac, and Jacob are irrevocable (Rom 11:29). God's love for Israel is deep and eternal. The New Testament continues this narrative by showing how Jesus is the fulfillment of the promises made to Israel, and how the church, made up of Jew and gentile alike, carries forward God's mission.

Israel and the End of Days

Amillennialism recognizes Israel's unique place as God's chosen nation, honors her right to exist, and calls for fervent prayer for her salvation. It understands that the kingdom promised to Israel is realized spiritually in Christ and expanded through the church, but this does not erase Israel's identity or purpose.

Rejecting amillennialism solely because it does not endorse a literal, future national kingdom for Israel overlooks the theological richness and biblical faithfulness of this view. It also misses the opportunity to appreciate how amillennialism harmonizes the Old and New Testaments, emphasizing the continuity of God's redemptive work without divorcing Israel from the broader story of salvation.

Rather than rejection, amillennialism deserves careful study and respectful engagement—especially in conversations about Israel. It challenges us to see God's promises fulfilled in Jesus and calls us to pray, watch, and live faithfully as part of his kingdom people today.

May this understanding foster unity rather than division, hope rather than despair, and faithfulness rather than fear as we anticipate the glorious return of our Lord and Savior.

As we move forward in this journey through eschatology, remember that the question of Israel's role is not merely an academic puzzle but a living, breathing reality with eternal implications. Whether one embraces amillennialism, dispensationalism, or another view, our hope remains anchored in the person and work of Jesus Christ. The differences we explore are opportunities to deepen our understanding, sharpen our faith, and encourage one another in love. Ultimately, the end of the ages will bring the full and final fulfillment of all God's promises—a new heaven, a new earth, and the eternal reign of the King. Until then, may we watch with hope, pray with passion, and live with unwavering faith.

Chapter 6

Objections to the Hybrid Approach

Objection 1: "Your View Is a Contradiction— You Can't Mix Dispensationalism with Amillennialism"

Critics Say:

DISPENSATIONALISM AND AMILLENNIALISM ARE fundamentally incompatible. Dispensationalism typically requires a literal, future earthly kingdom for Israel, a distinct plan for Israel and the church, and often a pre-tribulation rapture. Amillennialism teaches that the kingdom is spiritual and currently fulfilled in the church, often viewing Israel's promises as fulfilled in Christ and the church rather than in a literal future nation.

Response:

At first glance, it may seem impossible to combine these two perspectives. But Scripture and history suggest that the truth about God's redemptive plan is often richer and more complex than our theological categories allow. The approach I advocate—dispensational amillennialism—is a sincere attempt to hold these biblical tensions together rather than forcing the text into rigid boxes.

The Pharisees, Sadducees, and Zealots: An Ancient Analogy for Today's Eschatology

In the first century, Jesus ministered among a diverse Jewish population, including Pharisees, Sadducees, and Zealots. Each group had a distinct view of God, Israel, and the Messiah:

- **Pharisees** emphasized strict adherence to the law and believed in resurrection and angels, focusing on spiritual purity and the coming kingdom.
- **Sadducees** denied resurrection and angels, emphasizing temple worship and the priestly caste, often downplaying afterlife.
- **Zealots** sought a militant political liberation, expecting a Messiah to overthrow Rome and restore Israel's national kingdom by force.

None of these groups fully grasped the full truth of Jesus' mission. Jesus corrected and challenged them all but also used their sincere hopes and beliefs to reveal the fuller reality of the kingdom—one that was both "already" inaugurated through his first coming and "not yet" fulfilled in His return.

In the same way, modern eschatological systems each contain partial truths and errors:

- Dispensationalism rightly honors Israel's national role and God's ongoing covenants, emphasizing a literal fulfillment of promises and a future earthly kingdom.
- Amillennialism rightly emphasizes Christ's spiritual reign now and the church as the kingdom's present manifestation, avoiding overly literalistic expectations.

Neither system perfectly captures the full biblical narrative. Just as Jesus' first coming fulfilled but also transcended the hopes of the Pharisees, Sadducees, and Zealots, so the second coming and the kingdom will fulfill and transcend our current theological expectations.

Embracing Biblical Tensions with Humility

The kingdom is both "already" and "not yet." God's promises to Israel remain irrevocable (Rom 11:29), yet the kingdom Jesus inaugurated is spiritual and present in his church (Eph 1:22-23). These realities coexist in tension.

Dispensational amillennialism attempts to hold these tensions faithfully:

- affirming Israel's continuing role in God's plan, including future prophetic fulfillment;
- upholding the present spiritual reign of Christ and the church's identity as his kingdom people; and
- acknowledging end-time events like the "little while" (Rev 20) and a future deception involving a rebuilt temple, which differ from classical amillennialism's expectations.

This approach invites believers to step beyond rigid categories and recognize the depth and complexity of God's unfolding redemptive work.

A Call to Unity Without Uniformity

Just as Jesus called for repentance, faith, and love among his contemporaries with differing views, we, too, must hold our eschatological convictions with charity and openness. The second coming is mysterious, majestic, and beyond full human comprehension. Recognizing that the full truth likely lies somewhere in the middle—not in extremes—fosters unity instead of division, balance instead of extremes. It calls us to live faithfully in hope, watchfulness, and prayer while awaiting the King's return.

Objections to the Hybrid Approach

Objection 2: "You Expect a Third Temple, but That's a Dispensational Hallmark, Not Amillennial"

Critics Say:

Expecting a literal third temple to be rebuilt before Christ's return is a distinctly dispensational idea and contradicts the amillennial understanding that the temple is now the church, the spiritual dwelling place of God. How can you reconcile this expectation with amillennial theology?

Response:

This objection assumes that the rebuilding of a third temple must signify a millennial earthly kingdom or the full restoration of Israel's national worship system. However, my view—while acknowledging the temple's reconstruction—is nuanced and distinct from classic dispensational expectations.

The Third Temple as a Prophetic Sign of Deception, Not Fulfillment

I hold that the possible rebuilding of a third temple during the "little while" described in Rev 20:3, 7–10 is not the inauguration of Christ's kingdom on earth. Instead, it serves as a tool for satanic deception during the final rebellion against God.

- **Biblical Basis:**

    Jesus warned of the "abomination of desolation" in Matt 24:15, which signals a defilement of the holy place by lawlessness, not a holy restoration. The temple in this context becomes a focal point of end-times apostasy and the man of lawlessness's reign (2 Thess 2:3–4).

Revelation 20's "little while" describes a brief period when Satan is released to deceive the nations—this aligns with a counterfeit temple functioning as a religious hub for false worship and the antichrist's global system.

- **Shared Recognition of Deception:**

Interestingly, both classic dispensationalists and my view would at least initially recognize the rebuilding of a third temple as a significant prophetic sign—not necessarily a cause for celebration but a warning.

The writer of Hebrews reminds us that "the blood of bulls and goats could never take away sins" (Heb 10:4), underscoring the ultimate insufficiency of any temple sacrifices apart from Christ's perfect atoning work. Thus, even if a third temple is built, it cannot accomplish salvation or inaugurate God's kingdom—it is, at best, a shadow of what has been fulfilled in Jesus.

The Temple and the Church: Spiritual vs. Physical Realities

Amillennialism rightly teaches that Christ's church is now the temple—the dwelling place of God's Spirit (1 Cor 3:16; Eph 2:21-22). This spiritual temple does not exclude the possibility of a physical temple being built but interprets its function and significance differently.

- The physical temple's rebuilding is not an indication of God's blessing or kingdom fulfillment but a sign of the intensification of rebellion before Christ's final judgment.
- This view maintains the centrality of Christ as the true temple (John 2:19-21) and rejects any notion that a human-constructed temple could supplant the sufficiency of his work.

The Third Temple and Eschatological Caution

This perspective encourages discernment and caution:

- It warns against prematurely celebrating or endorsing the temple's construction as a sign of hope.
- It calls the church to be watchful for signs of deception and apostasy associated with it.
- It remains anchored in the certainty that Christ will return to consume all opposition with heavenly fire (Rev 20:9–10).

Objection 3: "Your Emphasis on Israel's National Role Undermines the Gospel of Grace"

Critics Say:

Focusing heavily on Israel's national identity and future can risk confusing the gospel by shifting emphasis from salvation through Jesus Christ alone to ethnic or political nationalism. Some worry this emphasis may lead to legalism or exclusion of the gentile believer's equal standing in Christ.

Response:

This objection raises an important pastoral and theological concern, but it misunderstands the nature and heart of my view.

The Historical and Prophetic Significance of Israel's Land

The land of Israel has been the stage for some of the most pivotal events in redemptive history:

- It was the land God promised to Abraham and his descendants (Gen 12:7; 15:18–21).
- It was the place where the patriarchs lived and where God established his covenant people.
- The temple stood there as the center of worship and sacrifice (2 Chr 7:16).
- It is where the Messiah, Jesus Christ, was born, lived, died, and rose again (Luke 2:4–7; John 19:16–18; Matt 28:6).
- Jerusalem is called the city of the great king (Ps 48:2) and the place to which all nations will come in the messianic age (Zech 8:20–23).

Given these monumental events, it is not unreasonable to anticipate that future significant prophetic events will also occur in this land, as Scripture repeatedly points to its ongoing importance (Zech 12:2–3; Ezek 37:21–22).

Israel's National Role Highlights the Glory of God's Grace

Far from undermining grace, Israel's history and future role magnify the amazing grace of God:

- The Jewish people were the ones who crucified the Lord of glory (1 Cor 2:8). Yet, God's plan of salvation is extended to them as well as to gentiles (Rom 11:15).
- The apostle Paul expresses deep sorrow for Israel's unbelief while holding onto hope: "I have great sorrow and unceasing anguish in my heart. For I could wish that I myself were cursed and cut off from Christ for the sake of my people, those of my own race" (Rom 9:2–3).
- Paul also writes that "all Israel will be saved" (Rom 11:26), emphasizing God's mercy and the power of the gospel to reach even those who once rejected the Messiah.

Salvation by Grace, Not Ethnicity or Nationality

- Salvation remains by grace alone through faith in Jesus Christ, for all people, Jew and gentile alike (Eph 2:8–9; Gal 3:28).
- Israel's role in God's redemptive plan is unique, but it does not confer automatic salvation. Personal faith in Christ is essential.

Praying and Hope for Israel without Political Nationalism

- The biblical command to pray for the peace of Jerusalem (Ps 122:6) and to intercede for Israel's salvation is a spiritual act of obedience, not political endorsement.
- The church is called to love all nations and proclaim the gospel universally, recognizing that God's promises to Israel are part of a broader redemptive story that culminates in Christ.

Objection 4: "Your 'Little While' Concept Is Too Speculative and Lacks Clear Biblical Support"

Critics Say:

The idea of a "little while" where Satan is released and a temple is rebuilt is reading too much into Rev 20. They argue that this is speculative and not supported by straightforward exegesis, making it an uncertain or questionable interpretation.

Response:

The "little while" mentioned in Rev 20:3 and 20:7 is a brief but significant period that deserves careful attention. While some aspects remain mysterious, there is solid biblical support to understand this as a real, future time of satanic release and deception prior to the final judgment.

Biblical Basis for the "Little While"

- **Revelation 20:3, 7:** The text explicitly states that Satan will be bound for a thousand years and then released "for a little while." The phrasing indicates a deliberate, limited period after the millennium (whether understood literally or figuratively).

- **Purpose of the Release:** Satan's release serves to "deceive the nations" (v. 8), gathering them for a final rebellion against God. This fits with other Scripture portraying a last-ditch rebellion before Christ's ultimate victory (e.g., Dan 11:36–45; 2 Thess 2:8–12).

Connecting the "Little While" to Prophetic Themes

- This period aligns with the "great tribulation" and the rise of the man of lawlessness (antichrist), who will deceive many and exalt himself against God (2 Thess 2:3–4).
- Jesus' warnings in Matt 24 about false messiahs and signs of deception prepare believers to expect intensified apostasy in the end times.

Objections to the Hybrid Approach

A Responsible Balance of Mystery and Clarity

- While the "little while" invites questions about exact timing and duration, it is biblically grounded as a future event involving satanic deception and final rebellion.
- It resists overly speculative interpretations by focusing on the clear biblical text and the broader narrative of God's ultimate triumph.

Theological Significance

- The "little while" underscores God's sovereignty—even in the midst of satanic deception. Satan's power is limited and ultimately defeated.
- It calls the church to vigilance, prayer, and faithfulness during times of spiritual conflict.

Objection 5: "Your View Creates Confusion and Division by Mixing Views"

Critics Say:

By blending dispensational and amillennial elements, your hybrid approach confuses believers and complicates eschatological understanding. Instead of providing clarity, it risks creating more division within the church by mixing theological categories traditionally seen as incompatible.

Response:

While this objection is understandable given the historical tensions between eschatological camps, my personal view actually seeks to *bring clarity and foster unity*, not confusion or division.

Clarity Through a Reasonable Explanation of Rebellion and Reign

- One of the strengths of this approach is that it offers a *more coherent explanation for how rebellion can exist simultaneously with Christ's reigning kingdom.*
- Rather than forcing a false either/or between the present reign of Christ and the reality of future satanic deception, this view acknowledges the *biblical tension* that both are true. Satan's binding and release (Rev 20) explain how evil persists under Christ's sovereign reign.
- This clarity helps believers understand *how Scripture harmonizes seemingly contradictory realities* without ignoring or spiritualizing the text.

Unity Around Shared Hope

- Importantly, this view underscores that *all orthodox eschatological positions agree on the core hope: Christ will return, defeat evil, and establish his eternal kingdom.*
- The division is often about the timing or the sequence of events—the *"when" not the "if."* Emphasizing this shared hope can reduce division and encourage mutual respect.
- The hybrid view encourages *unity by focusing on our common faith in Christ's victorious return* rather than insisting on rigid labels.

Pastoral and Theological Benefits

- This perspective equips pastors and teachers with a *balanced framework* to explain complex end-times realities without oversimplifying or alienating believers.

Objections to the Hybrid Approach

- It invites believers to live in *hopeful anticipation and watchfulness*, grounded in Scripture's full counsel.

A Call to Charity and Humility

- Theological diversity should not fracture the body of Christ but rather enrich it.
- Holding to this nuanced view requires humility, recognizing that *God's plans and timing are ultimately beyond full human comprehension.*

Objection 6: "What About the Promises and Prophecies Traditionally Understood to Be Fulfilled in a Literal Millennium?"

Summary of the Concern:

Many believers point to Old Testament promises—such as peace in Jerusalem, the lion lying down with the lamb, justice flowing like a river, a rebuilt temple, and long life—as being clearly, physically fulfilled during a future thousand-year reign of Christ on earth. These prophecies seem too specific and grand to be merely symbolic or spiritualized. Critics of your view may ask, *if you say the millennium is now, where are these things?*

Response: A Theological and Biblical Reframing

The Kingdom Has Come, but Not in Full

Many of the prophecies commonly associated with a literal millennium *have already begun to be fulfilled*—but not in the way people expected. Jesus said, "My kingdom is not of this world" (John 18:36), and he inaugurated that kingdom at his first coming. The *miracles, healings, and teachings of Christ were foretastes* of the restoration spoken of in the prophets. As Heb 2:8 notes, "At present, we do not yet see everything in subjection to him." That doesn't mean Christ isn't reigning—it means his reign is still unfolding.

Prophetic Language Is Often Poetic, Not Literal

Much of the language in Isaiah, Ezekiel, and Zechariah was *apocalyptic and symbolic*, reflecting God's promises through *the imagery and expectations of ancient Israel*. Just as "every mountain will be brought low" (Isa 40:4) is not about topography, neither is "the lion shall lie down with the lamb" (Isa 11:6) necessarily zoological. These are *pictures of peace and harmony under the reign of the Messiah*, which have *begun now in the church* and will be fully realized in the new heavens and new earth.

The Literal-Future Fulfillment Assumes a Gap That Isn't There

Many of the prophecies believed to require a literal millennium—such as a renewed temple, perfect justice, or Israel's national restoration—*find fulfillment either in Christ or in the new creation*. For example,

- **Ezekiel's Temple (Ezek 40–48)** finds its fulfillment in *Christ himself*, the true temple (John 2:19), and *in his body, the church* (Eph 2:21).

- **Jeremiah's New Covenant (Jer 31)** is *already in effect* (Heb 8).

- *The regathering of Israel* is both *physical and spiritual*, with Jews and gentiles united in one people of God (Rom 9–11, Eph 2).

Objections to the Hybrid Approach

The New Earth Is the Final Fulfillment, Not an Earthly Millennium

Revelation 21–22 shows that the *true fulfillment of Old Testament prophetic hope* is not a temporary thousand-year phase on this fallen earth, but *a renewed cosmos—free of death, sin, and Satan.* Many of the promises people assign to a literal millennium (perfect peace, God dwelling with his people, nations bringing their glory to Jerusalem, etc.) *actually appear in the description of the new heavens and new earth,* not in Rev 20.

This View Doesn't Deny the Fulfillment of These Promises—It Repositions Them

Rather than being *unfulfilled*, the promises are either:

- **already fulfilled** in Christ and the church (e.g., the indwelling presence of God),
- **being fulfilled** now (e.g., the gospel going to the nations, peace among enemies),
- or **awaiting final fulfillment** in the eternal kingdom (e.g., perfect peace, resurrection bodies, full glory of God's presence).

The amillennial understanding, and especially this hybrid view, doesn't reject these prophecies—it *anchors them in Christ and stretches them toward the eternal horizon,* rather than parking them in a temporary kingdom that Scripture never fully elaborates.

Closing Thought for This Objection

Instead of asking, *"Where is the literal fulfillment?"* perhaps we should ask, *"Where is Christ in this promise?"* The answer will always lead us to *a richer, more Christ-centered understanding of prophecy.* He is the key to every covenant, every promise, and every prophecy.

Objection 7: Doesn't the Advancement of the Gospel and Satan's Binding Sound More Like Postmillennialism Than Premillennialism?

This is a fair and thoughtful question, especially for those familiar with the broad categories of eschatology. The idea that Satan is presently bound (Rev 20:1–3) and that the gospel is going forward with increasing global impact often seems to align more closely with **postmillennialism**, which teaches that the world will be increasingly transformed by the gospel before Christ returns. In contrast, **premillennialism** tends to expect a global decline and worsening conditions before Jesus returns to establish a literal thousand-year kingdom.

But here is the key distinction: in **dispensational amillennialism**, the binding of Satan does not mean his total inactivity or the eradication of evil from the world. Instead, it refers to a specific kind of limitation—namely, that *he can no longer deceive the nations in the same way he once did* (Rev 20:3). Prior to Christ's first coming, the truth of God was largely confined to Israel. The gentile nations were, as Paul described, "without God and without hope in the world" (Eph 2:12). But after Christ's death, resurrection, and the outpouring of the Spirit at Pentecost, the gospel began to spread beyond Israel to the ends of the earth.

In that sense, this present age can be characterized as a time of *gospel advancement* and *spiritual conquest*, not because the world is becoming a utopia but because *Christ is actively drawing people from every tribe, tongue, and nation into his kingdom* (Rev 7:9). The victory is spiritual, not political.

Where postmillennialism sees a gradual Christianization of all culture and nations prior to Christ's return, *dispensational amillennialism sees gospel expansion in the midst of tribulation and opposition*, not necessarily resulting in global dominance but in global witness. As Jesus said in Matt 24:14, "This gospel of the kingdom will be proclaimed throughout the whole world as a testimony to all nations, and then the end will come."

Rather than contradicting amillennialism, the gospel's spread actually *confirms the binding of Satan*. He is restrained from preventing the global spread of the gospel, even though he remains active in persecution, temptation, and deception at the personal and local levels.

So yes, this view does overlap with postmillennialism in affirming Christ's current reign and gospel success—but it *diverges sharply in tone and expectation*. Amillennialism (especially the version presented here) does not expect a golden age of peace or Christian political rule. Instead, it anticipates increasing tension between the church and the world, a final surge of satanic deception when the restraint is lifted (the "little while"), and Christ's return to bring judgment and the new heavens and earth.

The gospel's advancement is *not a sign that we're entering a utopia* but that *God is keeping His promise to Abraham*, blessing the nations through his seed—Jesus Christ (Gal 3:16).

Objection 8: "What About the Rapture of the Church?"

Critics Ask:

If your view blends dispensationalism and amillennialism, what happens to the rapture? Traditional dispensationalists affirm a pre-tribulation rapture distinct from the second coming, while amillennialists typically see no rapture event at all. Doesn't your view remove one of the most cherished hopes of modern evangelical believers?

Response:

This objection matters deeply to many faithful Christians. The rapture—our being caught up to meet Christ in the air—is not just a theological position for many but a powerful emotional anchor in times of uncertainty. I don't dismiss it. In fact, I affirm the strong possibility of such an event—but *I do not treat it as a guaranteed biblical certainty*. Rather, I hold the position that *a rapture-like event may occur, and if it does, it will align with Christ's visible return at the end of the age.*

Let's break this down carefully.

1. A Biblical Possibility, Not a Certainty

- I do not hold to a dogmatic, guaranteed rapture doctrine as classically described in dispensational circles.

- Instead, I see the rapture as a *theological possibility* that aligns logically with several texts (e.g., 1 Thess 4:16–17), and fits within a coherent end-times framework that does not require two separate returns of Christ.

- The idea of the church being "caught up" to meet the Lord is clearly taught in Scripture. The *timing, purpose,* and *nature* of that event, however, are far more debated—and are *not definitively laid out as a separate event from Christ's second coming.*

Meeting the King, Then Coming With Him

- In 1 Thess 4, the word for "meet" (ἀπάντησις, *apantēsis*) describes a welcoming party—like a delegation that meets a king outside the city and escorts him in.

- In this light, I believe it's *entirely reasonable* to interpret the rapture not as a departure from Earth but as a meeting of Christ in the air followed by an immediate return to Earth in glory (see also **Acts 28:15**).

- This fits naturally with **Rev 19**, where Christ descends with the armies of heaven (which would now include his resurrected saints), ready to bring final judgment.

Objections to the Hybrid Approach

Why It Still Inspires Hope

- Some may ask, "But doesn't this take away our 'blessed hope'?" (Titus 2:13). Not at all.
- Whether the church is caught up and returns with Christ in an instant or remains on Earth until his coming, *our hope is not in the method of rescue, but in the Man who rescues.*
- The true "blessed hope" is not escape—it is *Jesus himself.* The timing and logistics are secondary to the joy of being united with him forever.

A View That Bridges the Gap

- For those who cherish the idea of a rapture, this view offers a *reasonable reconciliation:*
  o It neither dismisses the catching up of believers as myth,
  o nor insists upon a two-stage return or a secret pre-tribulation escape.
- Instead, it places the "rapture" (if it occurs) at *the end of this present age,* as part of the *glorious return of Christ,* visible to all.
- In this sense, it *respects both the language of Scripture and the longings of many believers,* without creating theological dissonance.

Tribulation Does Not Mean Abandonment

- The church may go through tribulation, but that does not mean she is forgotten. Just as God protected Israel through Egypt's plagues and Noah through the flood, so *he sustains his people in hardship.*

- Revelation repeatedly shows the saints overcoming—not by fleeing, but by faith, perseverance, and the blood of the Lamb (see Rev 12:11).

Final Thought

So do I believe in the rapture? *Possibly*. Do I believe it is certain? *No*. But I do believe the return of Christ is certain, and if a rapture event coincides with his return, it will not contradict anything in Scripture—it will *magnify his glory*. This framework allows believers to hope without demanding precision on what Scripture does not make explicit. It allows curiosity and caution to walk hand in hand.

Conclusion: A Faith That Engages, Not Escapes

After walking through the major objections to a dispensational amillennial perspective—including those that come from both traditional amillennial and dispensational camps—it becomes clear that the goal of this view is not to rewrite biblical prophecy but to refine how we understand it in light of Scripture, history, and the nature of Christ's already-not-yet kingdom.

In many ways, the tension surrounding eschatological debates reveals something deeper than theological preference. It exposes how we view the Bible's unfolding drama, how we interpret the nature of the church, and how we expect God to fulfill his promises to Israel and the world. But even deeper still, it challenges how we live in the present while longing for the future.

Some may say this "middle ground" creates confusion—but I argue it brings clarity. For instance, seeing Satan's release not as an arbitrary evil eruption but as a permitted and prophesied event offers a more coherent explanation for the worldwide deception we are warned about. How could the nations be so misled? Because, if the church is taken up or removed from its earthly influence—even

Objections to the Hybrid Approach

temporarily—the absence of truth-bearing believers would leave the world vulnerable to the lie. A rebuilt temple in Jerusalem, revered by both Jews and many Christians, could serve as a focal point for global deception, especially when coupled with signs and wonders and false claims of messianic fulfillment. It makes sense. It's biblically plausible. It's not dogma—but it is discernment.

We've also addressed the common objection that a spiritual millennium undermines the literal promises given to Israel. But upon further inspection, those promises don't have to be interpreted in opposition to grace—they can be seen as amplifying it. Consider how astounding it is that the very nation who rejected their Messiah (Acts 2:36, "You crucified the Lord of Glory") is still deeply woven into the redemptive tapestry. God's faithfulness isn't nullified by their rebellion; rather, his mercy is magnified. The gospel doesn't erase Israel—it explains her. From Genesis to Revelation, Israel is both a real people and a symbol of God's covenant mercy. The church does not replace Israel; it fulfills and expands her reach to the ends of the earth.

Others object to the notion that these views can coexist. But history teaches us otherwise. Even in the first century, Jesus encountered a variety of Jewish sects—Pharisees, Sadducees, Essenes, Zealots. None were completely right. None were completely wrong. Each grasped part of the truth but missed the fullness of the picture. In the same way, perhaps the debate surrounding the second coming mirrors the debates before the first. No one anticipated a suffering servant and a conquering king in one man. Today, we may be struggling with a similar paradox: a spiritual reign now and a victorious return soon.

Still others may object to the idea that the church could be raptured—not because the Bible clearly refutes it but because it doesn't clearly confirm it. And I agree. I'm not dogmatic about a rapture in the traditional sense, but I'm not dismissive of it either. It makes theological sense that Christ could remove his bride before unleashing final judgment and releasing Satan for a "little while." This would not only spare the faithful from wrath but would explain how deception could spread globally without resistance. Without truth-bearers, error reigns. The rapture of the Church would also make the world look exactly like it did in the Old Testament before Christ. A dark world with nearly every nation deceived, and being deceived. A world looking for hope, a messiah, that would gladly embrace an Antichrist type figure.

Let's be honest: the confusion surrounding the end times isn't because the Bible is unclear; it's because we bring our systems, expectations, and assumptions to it. But here's the encouraging part—every major eschatological view agrees on one central hope: Jesus is coming again. That's the unshakable promise. The "when" may be debated, but the "Who" is not. We are not waiting for an event; we are waiting for a person.

And this is why this conversation matters. Not just for scholars or prophecy buffs but for pastors, teachers, and everyday Christians who are trying to make sense of the chaos in the world. We live in a time where deception is rampant, morality is collapsing, and anxiety is on the rise. People are hungry for hope. If our theology doesn't offer that, it's not worth having.

Dispensational amillennialism, as I've proposed it, doesn't demand you reject your past understanding—it invites you to refine it. It holds the Bible in highest esteem, acknowledges the reality of Israel, honors the trajectory of redemptive history, and offers a sensible framework for the church's mission now and in the days to come.

So where do we go from here?

We must remember that prophecy was not given to puff up our intellects but to prepare our hearts. We're not called to merely speculate but to shepherd. And that leads us to the next crucial step: how should pastors, leaders, and church members approach these theological matters in a way that builds up rather than tears down?

Chapter 7 will focus on the pastoral implications of these truths—because theology divorced from love leads to division. But theology rooted in Christ produces discernment, courage, and compassion. As shepherds of God's people, our calling is not just to rightly divide the word—but to rightly apply it in a way that fuels worship, hope, and mission.

Our goal is not to be right but to be ready. Not to win arguments but to win souls. And so we continue—not with pride but with open Bibles, open hearts, and eyes fixed on the One who is coming soon.

Chapter 7

A Pastoral Approach to Eschatology

Introduction: A Personal Confession and a Pastoral Concern

I WAS BORN AND raised in church. From my earliest memories, the Bible was always present. I read it regularly. I listened to sermons, attended Sunday school, youth group, and eventually ministry training. I read Christian books, devotionals, and theology. I sat under dozens of pastors—many of them faithful, godly men who loved the word of God and took their calling seriously.

And yet, for all those years, I only ever heard one eschatological view presented: the dispensational premillennial perspective. It was treated as fact, as settled doctrine—as if the only real question was *how soon* it would all happen. I never even knew there were other options. No one ever said, "Some Christians interpret these things differently." No one said, "There are multiple historic views of the end times." No one said, "Here's what others believe, and here's why."

Looking back, I find that both concerning and—if I'm honest—a little infuriating. This is an important doctrine. It's not peripheral. Eschatology speaks to the return of our King, the resurrection of the dead, the final judgment, and the renewal of all

A Pastoral Approach to Eschatology

things. These aren't small matters. And yet, despite its significance, the only narrative I was given was one narrow path. That should concern us.

What troubles me more is this: no one seems to acknowledge that even pastors and professors have knowledge limitations. As believers, we are often handed packaged theology without any indication that faithful Christians—some far wiser than us—have held differing views. We are rarely told that the topic is complex. Rarely told that godly men have wrestled with these questions for centuries. Rarely told that it's OK to wrestle with them ourselves.

But the people in our churches deserve better. They deserve to know the truth—that there are multiple views that have been taken seriously across church history, and that many of those views are held by Bible-believing, Christ-honoring Christians today. They deserve to know that pastors, too, are still learning. That we don't have every answer, and that's OK.

That realization reshaped how I view my role as a pastor. I no longer see myself as someone who must always provide definitive answers. I see myself now as a shepherd who guides people into Scripture, opens doors for theological curiosity, and invites honest exploration—even when the conclusions aren't all the same.

This chapter is the most important to me in this entire book, not because I think I have the perfect view on the end times—I don't. But because I want to call pastors and teachers to a higher standard of theological honesty and humility. We don't serve our congregations well by pretending there's only one interpretation that matters. Nor do we honor Christ when we elevate our certainty over unity or use prophecy charts as litmus tests for orthodoxy.

What I hope to offer here is a practical, pastoral road map, not just for how to *teach* eschatology but for how to *shepherd people through it*. This means presenting multiple views without confusion. It means holding firm convictions without arrogance. It means creating environments where dialogue is welcome and phrases like "I believe this because . . ." and "Others believe this because . . ." are heard often.

Imagine the impact on a young believer hearing for the first time that their pastor doesn't claim to know it all—but trusts the Word enough to let it speak. Imagine the freedom that comes from realizing that we can disagree on the *timing* of Christ's return while being fully united in hope that *he will return*. Imagine the maturity that can grow when the church becomes a place of theological exploration, not just indoctrination.

The goal of this chapter is to help foster that kind of environment. One where pastors lead with humility, clarity, and gospel-centered focus. One where eschatology is not a battleground, but a classroom—where Christ is exalted, hope is ignited, and every conversation ends with worship, not war.

Let's teach the truth. Let's teach all of it. And let's never be afraid to say, "This is what I believe. Here's why. But others believe this, and here's why." In doing so, we honor the truth, honor our people, and most importantly, honor Christ.

Teaching the Whole Counsel of God

One of the apostle Paul's final charges in his ministry was this: "I did not shrink from declaring to you the whole counsel of God" (Acts 20:27). That statement has always struck me as deeply pastoral. It's not just about preaching regularly. It's about preaching *honestly*. It's about declaring all that God has said—not just what is easy to understand or what we've been told by others but the *whole* of divine truth, even the parts we wrestle with ourselves.

If we are to follow in Paul's footsteps, we must teach the whole counsel of God—including eschatology. And not just one version of it.

The Weight of Responsibility

As pastors and teachers, we bear an incredible responsibility. James 3:1 warns us that not many should become teachers, for we will be judged more strictly. That judgment includes how we handle

Scripture—not just in content but in *scope*. It's not enough to teach only what we were taught. Nor is it enough to teach only what we've personally come to believe. We are responsible to present the full range of biblical teaching, especially in areas where faithful, Spirit-filled believers have historically disagreed.

When we teach eschatology as if there is only one biblical option, we run the risk of doing two great disservices:

- First, we create confusion when sincere believers encounter other perspectives for the first time—often from skeptics or critics.
- Second, we rob our people of the rich theological tradition that can actually *strengthen* their hope rather than weaken it.

The goal is not to overwhelm them with charts and timelines. The goal is to faithfully shepherd them toward a deeper trust in the promises of God and a firmer hope in the return of Christ.

Don't Be a Gatekeeper—Be a Guide

There is a subtle danger in pastoral ministry: the temptation to become a gatekeeper of "acceptable" interpretations. Some do this unintentionally, others quite deliberately. Either way, it reduces the church's theology to a narrow funnel, often shaped more by denominational tradition or personal preference than by biblical breadth.

But shepherds aren't called to guard *traditions*—we're called to guard *truth*. And truth demands that we give our people the tools to study, weigh, and discern for themselves.

Instead of saying, *"This is the only way to understand Revelation 20,"* what if we said, *"Here are the major ways faithful Christians have understood this passage—and here's why I believe the one I do."*

Rather than eliminating discussion, that kind of statement invites it. Rather than creating anxiety, it builds maturity. Rather than controlling people's conclusions, it cultivates confidence in

Scripture and in the Holy Spirit's ability to lead each believer into truth.

How This Looks in Practice

Teaching the whole counsel of God in this area may feel intimidating, especially if you're preaching to a congregation that's only ever known one eschatological view. But it doesn't have to be disruptive—it can be *freeing*.

Here are some practical ways this might look:

- **Preach Through Apocalyptic Texts with Honesty**—When preaching from Daniel, Matt 24, or Revelation, acknowledge the variety of interpretations. Say, *"Some believe this refers to a future antichrist, others believe this has already been fulfilled. Let's look at the text together."*

- **Use Clear Language Like "I Believe . . ." and "Others Believe . . ."**—This phrase is gold. It lets your people know where you stand but also opens the door for gracious dialogue. It's humble, honest, and respectful.

- **Invite Guest Teachers Who Hold Different Views**—If your church setting allows it, consider hosting a forum or class with multiple perspectives. Not for debate but for learning. It models unity in diversity and shows that truth isn't threatened by honest discussion.

- **Equip Your Teachers and Leaders**—Don't just leave this to the pulpit. Train your small group leaders, Sunday school teachers, and youth workers to be aware of the main eschatological views and how to present them accurately and fairly.

- **Create Safe Spaces for Questions**—This is huge. If your church isn't a safe place to say, *"I've always wondered if that's really what the Bible teaches,"* then you've unintentionally created a culture of silence and fear. Encourage questions. Invite wrestling. Be the first to say, *"I don't have all the answers, but let's search Scripture together."*

This is the kind of teaching that grows churches—not just in numbers, but in depth and maturity. When we teach the whole counsel of God, including the hard parts, we model trust in the word and trust in the Spirit's work within our people.

Let's not shrink back from this. Let's press in with boldness, humility, and grace.

Presenting All Major Views, Not Just One

One of the greatest barriers to healthy eschatological teaching in churches is the sense that there is only one "correct" view. This often leads to rigid teaching, fear of questions, and sometimes even judgment of those who hold different convictions. But the truth is, the history of Christian theology shows us a rich tapestry of perspectives—each shaped by Scripture, tradition, and earnest study.

As pastors, embracing this complexity is not a weakness; it's an invitation to deeper faith.

Why Present Multiple Views?

- **Strengthen Biblical Literacy**

    When we expose our congregations to various views—whether dispensational premillennialism, historic premillennialism, postmillennialism, or amillennialism—we deepen their understanding of Scripture. They learn to see the biblical texts from different angles and appreciate the nuances rather than settling for simplistic answers.

- **Build Spiritual Maturity**

    Encountering and wrestling with diverse views cultivates humility and discernment. It teaches believers to weigh arguments, ask good questions, and trust the Spirit's guidance. It prevents immature "tunnel vision" and prepares them for spiritual challenges.

- **Encourage Unity Amid Diversity**

    When we show that faithful Christians differ on eschatology, it reminds us that unity in the body doesn't require uniformity on every point. We can agree on the essentials—Christ's return, resurrection, judgment—and graciously accept differences on secondary matters.

How to Present Views Faithfully

Presenting multiple views is not about watering down truth or promoting relativism. It's about being faithful to Scripture *and* gracious to your listeners.

Here's a simple approach:

- **Define Each View Clearly**

    Give your people clear, concise descriptions of each major eschatological position. Avoid caricatures or straw men. For example:

    o *Dispensational premillennialism*: The belief in a future, literal thousand-year reign of Christ on earth following a pre-tribulation rapture.

    o *Historic premillennialism*: Christ's return will inaugurate a literal millennium, but there is no pre-tribulation rapture.

    o *Postmillennialism*: The kingdom of God will gradually increase on earth until Christ returns after a golden age of peace.

    o *Amillennialism*: The millennium is symbolic of Christ's present spiritual reign; his return will bring the final judgment and new creation.

- **Explain the Scriptural Support for Each**

    Present key verses and theological reasons each view offers for its position. This helps your people see that these views aren't just opinions—they are reasoned interpretations grounded in Scripture.

- **Share Historical and Contemporary Advocates**

   Tell stories about how respected church fathers, Reformers, and modern theologians have held each view. This builds respect for different positions.

- **Be Transparent About Your Conviction**

   After presenting the views, say something like, *"Personally, I believe [your view], because of [brief reasons]. But I want you to know that other Christians you respect may hold different views, and that's okay."*

Practical Benefits of This Approach

- **Prevent Surprises and Confusion**

   When people hear different views only outside the church—on social media, podcasts, or from friends—they can feel betrayed or confused. Presenting these views openly avoids that.

- **Foster Respectful Dialogue**

   Teaching multiple views creates a culture where differences are discussed respectfully, reducing judgment and division.

- **Encourage Personal Study and Growth**

   When people know there's more than one view, many will be inspired to study the Bible deeper and grow in faith.

A Word of Caution

This approach requires wisdom. You don't want to overwhelm people with details or create doubt about foundational truths. The key is *balance*: teach with confidence but also with openness.

Always keep Christ at the center. Make clear which doctrines are essential to salvation and which are open for debate.

Creating Space for Others to Share

The local church is not just a place for preaching; it's a community—a family—where God's people learn from one another. When it comes to complex and often divisive topics like eschatology, creating space for others to share their views isn't just a courtesy—it's a pastoral imperative.

Why Invite Multiple Voices?

- **It Models Humility and Openness**

  When pastors invite others to share, it shows that no one holds a monopoly on truth. This models Christlike humility and encourages believers to listen as well as speak.

- **It Enriches the Church's Understanding**

  Different teachers bring different emphases and insights. This broadens the church's theological horizons and helps avoid blind spots.

- **It Builds Unity in Diversity**

  A church culture that welcomes varied perspectives is less prone to factionalism. It reminds us that we are united by faith in Christ, not by uniformity in eschatology.

Practical Ways to Create Space

- **Guest Speakers and Panel Discussions**

  Invite pastors or scholars who hold differing eschatological views for a joint teaching event or panel. Frame it as a time of learning, not debate.

- **Small Group Conversations**

  Encourage leaders to facilitate open discussions in small groups, where people feel safer to ask questions and express doubts.

- **Q&A Sessions After Sermons**

  Allow time for questions after sermons on prophecy or end-times topics. Be prepared to say, "That's a great question. Let's explore it together."

- **Encourage Written Questions or Forums**

  Set up opportunities for congregants to submit questions anonymously if they're uncomfortable asking in public.

The Pastor's Role as Facilitator

Your role shifts from sole "expert" to *guide* and *facilitator*. This requires:

- **Listening Carefully**

  Hear the concerns, questions, and ideas of your people without judgment.

- **Encouraging Respectful Dialogue**

  Remind everyone that disagreement is natural and can be healthy when handled with love.

- **Providing Biblical Resources**

  Recommend books, articles, or sermons that present different views fairly.

- **Correcting Error Gently**

  If a teaching veers into unbiblical territory, address it lovingly and with Scripture, not with condemnation.

Stories from the Field

I've seen churches transformed when leaders invited dialogue on end-times topics. One pastor invited a panel of three speakers—each representing a different view—to teach and answer questions. The result? Many congregants were relieved to learn that Christians they respected held differing convictions and still loved Jesus deeply. The church grew in grace and theological maturity.

Creating space for others to share requires courage and intentionality, but the fruit is undeniable: a church better equipped to stand firm in hope and unity amid a confusing world.

In recent years, more and more churches have begun intentionally creating space for diverse theological perspectives on eschatology. Contrary to fears that this would lead to division or decline, the evidence suggests quite the opposite.

Many congregations report that when leaders openly present multiple views and encourage respectful dialogue, the church grows—not just in numbers but in depth of faith and unity of spirit. Rather than causing confusion or conflict, these honest conversations foster trust. Congregants appreciate hearing different viewpoints because it feels authentic and trustworthy in an age where cultural messages often distort truth.

People are hungry for honesty. When pastors admit that some doctrines are complex, that faithful Christians disagree, and that their own understanding is a journey rather than a destination, it resonates deeply. This transparency breaks down walls of skepticism and fear, inviting more people into meaningful engagement with Scripture.

This approach has also empowered many churches to develop stronger communities—where members feel safe asking tough questions, sharing doubts, and growing together in grace. It's a sign that the Spirit is working through humility and openness, drawing his people into a more mature and vibrant faith.

Modeling Humility from the Pulpit

As pastors, the way we communicate eschatological truths sets the tone for how our congregations engage these complex topics. Humility is key—not just humility before God but humility in how we present what we believe to our people. If you as a pastor do not share other non heretical views, your congregants will search them out. With TikTok, YouTube, and Instagram, all one has to do is give some time to another view and their feed will be filled with it. Sharing other views prevents confusion that will no doubt come through social media.

The Power of "I Believe..."

One simple yet powerful practice is to consistently use language like "I believe this because..." and "Others believe differently because..."

This phrasing does several important things:

- **It Honors Our Limitations**

  No pastor has perfect knowledge of the timing or details of the end times. Acknowledging that demonstrates integrity and models biblical humility.

- **It Opens Doors for Conversation**

  When people hear their pastor affirm other views, it reduces fear and defensiveness, making them more willing to ask questions and think critically.

- **It Avoids Imposing Certainty**

  We avoid the trap of treating one interpretation as the only truth, which can alienate those who hold different convictions.

Biblical Examples of Humble Leadership

Scripture models humility in leadership throughout:

- **Paul:** Though a great apostle, he confessed to not knowing all things fully (1 Cor 13:12). He presented truth with confidence but without arrogance.
- **Peter:** He sometimes struggled with understanding (Acts 10:28–29), yet was open to correction and growth.
- **Jesus himself:** He often used phrases like "You have heard it said . . ." and "But I say to you . . ." that both clarified and invited listeners to engage with his teaching thoughtfully.

These examples remind us that humility does not diminish authority; it strengthens credibility.

Avoiding Dogmatism

Dogmatic statements about eschatology often cause unnecessary division. When pastors say, "You must believe this or you are not a true Christian," they erect barriers instead of bridges.

Instead, pastors can teach firmly yet graciously, distinguishing between essentials of salvation and secondary doctrinal differences.

Embracing Questions and Doubts

Humility also means welcoming questions—even skeptical ones. When a congregant asks, "How can this be true?" or, "I don't understand that part," pastors should respond with patience and openness, not impatience or dismissal.

This cultivates a church culture where people can wrestle with hard questions honestly, leading to deeper faith.

Impact on the Church

When pastors model humility in teaching eschatology, the church is more likely to

- engage the Bible thoughtfully rather than superficially.
- foster unity despite differing views.
- grow in hope rooted in Christ rather than fear of speculation.
- develop a healthy curiosity about God's plan for the future.

Clarifying What Is Primary vs. Secondary

One of the greatest pastoral challenges when teaching eschatology is helping the church discern between *essential* doctrines that unite us and *secondary* doctrines, where faithful Christians may legitimately disagree.

What Must We Agree On?

At the core of biblical eschatology, there are several nonnegotiable truths every believer must affirm:

- **The return of Jesus Christ is certain and imminent** (Acts 1:11; Titus 2:13).
- **The resurrection of the dead will occur**—both the righteous and the unrighteous (John 5:28–29; 1 Cor 15).
- **There will be a final judgment** where Christ will judge all humanity (2 Cor 5:10; Rev 20:11–15).
- **God will renew all things** and establish his eternal kingdom (Rev 21–22).

These core truths form the foundation of Christian hope and faith. Disagreement on the details of the timing or nature of events should not shake these fundamentals.

What Can We Disagree On?

Secondary matters—where faithful Christians differ—include

- the timing and nature of the millennium (literal one thousand years vs. symbolic).
- The sequence of end-times events (pre-tribulation rapture, tribulation, millennium, final judgment).
- the interpretation of prophetic passages (literal vs. figurative).
- the role of Israel and the church in eschatology.

These differences arise from sincere biblical interpretation and have been held historically by godly men and women. It is important to affirm that holding any of these views does not threaten salvation or Christian fellowship.

Why This Clarification Matters

Without clear boundaries between primary and secondary doctrines,

- churches risk fracturing over nonessential issues.
- believers can become discouraged or confused.
- the gospel itself may be overshadowed by controversy.

Teaching This to the Church

Pastors should explicitly teach these distinctions so members understand

- salvation does not depend on agreeing with the pastor's eschatological view.
- disagreement on secondary issues is normal and permissible.
- the unity of the church is rooted in Christ, not in eschatological uniformity.

A practical way to communicate this is through teaching series, written statements, or FAQ guides that clearly explain what the church affirms and what it allows for freedom.

This clarity fosters a healthy church culture—one marked by both conviction and charity, faithfulness and grace.

Equipping the Church to Live, Not Just Speculate

Eschatology is not merely an intellectual exercise or a curiosity to satisfy. Its primary purpose is to shape how we live *now*—to give us hope, motivate holiness, and fuel mission.

Hope That Transforms

The promise of Christ's return is a powerful hope that encourages believers to persevere through trials (Rom 8:18–25), resist sin (Titus 2:11–14), and fix their eyes on the eternal (Heb 12:1–2).

When teaching eschatology, pastors must highlight that this hope isn't about escape from the present world but about God's ultimate victory and restoration.

Holiness and Urgency

Knowing that Christ will return and judge motivates believers to live holy lives (2 Pet 3:11–14). It fosters a sense of urgency—not panic but intentionality in how we use our time and resources.

This urgency shapes priorities, inspiring generosity, service, and evangelism.

Mission and Witness

Eschatology fuels mission. The gospel is not just good news for now but for eternity. We proclaim Christ's return as a reason for the world to repent and believe (2 Cor 5:10).

Teaching this should inspire churches to engage in outreach and discipleship with passion, knowing the clock is ticking.

Guard Against Speculation and Fear

While eschatology is important, pastors should guard against

- overemphasis on timelines or predictions.
- conspiracy theories that distract from the gospel.
- fear-driven teaching that leads to despair or escapism.

Encourage believers to focus on Christ, his word, and the mission he has given us today.

Practical Steps for Pastors

- Preach with gospel centrality, always pointing to Christ as the hope and Savior.
- Use eschatology to encourage perseverance, not anxiety.
- Incorporate practical applications in sermons and small groups.
- Model confident hope balanced with humble uncertainty about the details.

By equipping the church to live with hope and purpose rather than merely speculate, pastors fulfill one of their highest callings: leading God's people into abundant life in Christ here and now.

Shepherding People Through Shifting Views

It's not uncommon for believers—pastors included—to revisit and revise their eschatological views over time. Growth in understanding often brings new perspectives, questions, and even doubts. How pastors shepherd people through these transitions is crucial.

Normalize Growth and Change

Teach your congregation that spiritual growth includes wrestling with difficult doctrines. Just as faith matures, so can understanding. This helps remove stigma or fear when someone's views evolve.

Be Transparent About Your Journey

Share your own experiences with changing or refining your eschatological beliefs. This honesty builds trust and models humility. Sharing your own experiences with changing or refining your eschatological beliefs is more than just humility—it's a powerful way to build trust. When pastors are transparent about their theological journeys, struggles, and questions, it breaks down barriers between leader and congregation. People see that you are not infallible or distant but a fellow pilgrim on the path of faith.

This openness encourages congregants to come to you with their own doubts and questions, knowing they will be met with understanding rather than judgment. Transparency fosters an environment where honest conversation thrives, making it far more likely that your teaching will be received thoughtfully and with respect.

Provide Safe Spaces

Encourage small groups or counseling settings where people can discuss doubts or new insights without fear of judgment or exclusion.

Emphasize Unity in Christ

Remind the church that while views may differ or shift, the foundation—Jesus Christ—remains constant. Our identity in him transcends doctrinal details.

Address Confusion and Anxiety

Some believers may feel unsettled by shifting views. Pastors should patiently teach the essentials, reassure them of God's sovereignty, and offer pastoral care.

Encourage Ongoing Study

Motivate your people to keep studying Scripture and seeking God's guidance through prayer and fellowship, knowing that understanding unfolds over time.

Maintaining Gospel Centrality

No matter how complex or diverse eschatological views may be, the gospel must remain the heartbeat of every sermon and conversation about the end times.

Christ as the Center

Every teaching on eschatology must point to Jesus Christ—his finished work on the cross, his resurrection, and his promised return. Without this focus, end-times teaching risks becoming mere speculation or fear-mongering.

The Gospel as Our Hope

The gospel is the foundation of our hope in the future. It reminds us that salvation is by grace through faith (Eph 2:8–9), not by knowing prophetic timelines. This assurance guards against legalism or anxiety.

Preaching the Gospel to the Doubter and the Believer

Eschatology offers a unique opportunity to preach the gospel:

- To doubters, it can awaken the reality of judgment and the necessity of repentance.
- To believers, it renews hope and inspires holy living.

Avoiding Eschatological Idolatry

Warn against making eschatology itself an idol or a test of faith. Our trust must rest in Christ alone, not in any particular interpretation of prophecy.

Examples of Eschatological Idolatries

End-Times Obsession to the Exclusion of Daily Faithfulness: When believers become so consumed with predicting dates, watching for signs, or tracking prophetic fulfillments that they neglect their personal holiness, relationships, and service to others, this turns eschatology into a distraction rather than a motivation for godly living.

Prophecy as a Litmus Test for Orthodoxy: Judging other Christians' salvation or faithfulness based solely on their eschatological position. Saying things like, *"If you don't believe in a 'pre-trib' rapture, you're not a true Christian,"* elevates doctrine above the gospel and sows division.

Conspiracy Thinking and Fear-Mongering: Allowing eschatology to fuel paranoia, conspiracy theories, or anxiety about the future rather than hope in Christ can lead to isolation, despair, or radical behavior disconnected from biblical faith.

Speculation Over Scripture: Spending more time trying to decode cryptic signs, numbers, or political events than engaging with the clear and central truths of Scripture elevates human interpretation above the simplicity and sufficiency of the gospel.

Using Eschatology for Personal Gain: Some have used end-times teachings to manipulate followers—whether financially, politically, or socially—by playing on fears or promising secret knowledge.

Neglecting the Present Mission: Focusing exclusively on future events can cause neglect of the church's present mission of evangelism, discipleship, and mercy ministry.

Integrating Gospel Throughout

From sermon introduction to conclusion, weave gospel truths consistently, ensuring listeners leave with hearts anchored in Christ's saving work and eternal kingdom.

Conclusion and Final Encouragement

Teaching and shepherding through eschatological matters is both challenging and deeply rewarding. We wrestle with complex Scripture, diverse interpretations, and the weight of eternal hope. But as pastors, our greatest calling is to lead God's people with humility, clarity, and gospel-centeredness.

Throughout this chapter, we've seen that

- teaching the whole counsel of God honors Scripture and builds trust.
- presenting all major views fosters maturity and unity.
- creating space for others to share models humility and enriches the church.
- modeling humility ourselves invites honest dialogue and deeper faith.
- clarifying primary and secondary doctrines protects unity without compromising truth.
- equipping the church to live with hope guards against speculation and fear.
- shepherding people through shifting views nurtures grace and trust.
- maintaining gospel centrality keeps every discussion rooted in Christ's saving work.

- guarding against eschatological idolatries protects hearts from misdirected fear or obsession.

This pastoral approach does not promise perfect answers or immediate harmony. But it does promise a healthier, more vibrant church—one where believers can grow in hope, love, and unity amid the mysteries of God's plan. May God grant us wisdom, grace, and courage as we continue this vital work.

Appendix A

Exegesis of Key Texts from the Dispensational Amillennial Perspective

THIS APPENDIX PROVIDES A detailed examination of several key biblical passages foundational to the dispensational amillennial view. Each text is presented in full, followed by an exegetical analysis that highlights how it informs this perspective on eschatology, including the nature of the millennium, the role of Israel, the resurrection, and prophetic events such as the rebuilding of the third temple.

1. Revelation 20:1-6—The Binding of Satan and the "First Resurrection"

Passage (ESV)

> 1 Then I saw an angel coming down from heaven, holding in his hand the key to the bottomless pit and a great chain.
> 2 And he seized the dragon, that ancient serpent, who is the devil and Satan, and bound him for a thousand years,

3 and threw him into the pit, and shut it and sealed it over him, so that he might not deceive the nations any longer, until the thousand years were ended. After that he must be released for a little while.

4 Then I saw thrones, and seated on them were those to whom the authority to judge was committed. Also I saw the souls of those who had been beheaded for the testimony of Jesus and for the word of God, and those who had not worshiped the beast or its image and had not received its mark on their foreheads or their hands. They came to life and reigned with Christ for a thousand years.

5 The rest of the dead did not come to life until the thousand years were ended. This is the first resurrection.

6 Blessed and holy is the one who shares in the first resurrection! Over such the second death has no power, but they will be priests of God and of Christ, and they will reign with him for a thousand years.

Exegetical Notes

- The "thousand years" is symbolic of the present church age, during which Christ reigns spiritually through his church. This interpretation aligns with the apocalyptic genre's frequent use of symbolic numbers (see Dan 7; Rev 12).
- Satan's binding (v. 3) restricts his capacity to deceive the nations fully, thereby enabling the gospel's global spread (see 2 Cor 4:4; John 12:31).
- The "first resurrection" (v. 5) refers to a spiritual resurrection—believers being born again and united with Christ in the present age—distinct from the physical resurrection at Christ's second coming.
- The "rest of the dead" represents unbelievers who will be resurrected after the millennium at the final judgment.
- The bodily resurrection of believers is affirmed elsewhere (1 Thess 4:16–17; 1 Cor 15) and occurs visibly at Christ's return.

Exegesis of Key Texts from the Dispensational Amillennial Perspective

- This understanding preserves the hope of a future bodily resurrection while explaining Revelation's imagery in harmony with New Testament teaching on Christ's present reign.

2. Matthew 24:15—The "Abomination of Desolation" and the Third Temple

Passage (ESV)

> 15 So when you see the abomination of desolation spoken of by the prophet Daniel, standing in the holy place (let the reader understand),
> 16 then let those who are in Judea flee to the mountains.

Exegetical Notes

- Jesus' warning references Daniel's prophecy about a desecration of the "holy place."
- This "holy place" is interpreted as a future third temple yet to be rebuilt, distinct from the ancient temple destroyed in AD 70 and the current state of the temple mount.
- The "abomination of desolation" will be an act of sacrilege committed by the antichrist during the "little while" described in Rev 20:3, functioning as a sign of intensified tribulation and global deception (see 2 Thess 2:3-4; Dan 9:27).
- The temple serves as a central instrument in uniting many under the antichrist's rule, advancing his worldwide deception.
- Christ's return will decisively end this deception and the tribulation period by destroying the abomination and establishing his eternal kingdom.

3. 1 Thessalonians 4:16-17—The Resurrection and Rapture

Passage (ESV)

> **16** For the Lord himself will descend from heaven with a cry of command, with the voice of an archangel, and with the sound of the trumpet of God. And the dead in Christ will rise first.
> **17** Then we who are alive, who are left, will be caught up together with them in the clouds to meet the Lord in the air, and so we will always be with the Lord.

Exegetical Notes

- This passage describes the physical, bodily resurrection of believers and their being caught up ("raptured") to meet Christ at his return.

- It distinguishes the resurrection of deceased believers ("will rise first") from the transformation and gathering of living believers ("we who are alive").

- The timing aligns with the end of the church age and the "little while" in Rev 20, allowing for the possibility of a rapture before or during tribulation without insisting on a pre-tribulation position.

- The bodily nature of this event emphasizes the continuity of personal identity and the redemption believers will experience at Christ's return.

4. Romans 11:25-27—Israel's Partial Hardening and Salvation

Passage (ESV)

> **25** Lest you be wise in your own sight, I do not want you to be unaware of this mystery, brothers: a partial

hardening has come upon Israel, until the fullness of the Gentiles has come in.

26 And in this way all Israel will be saved, as it is written,
"The Deliverer will come from Zion,
he will banish ungodliness from Jacob";
27 "and this will be my covenant with them when I take away their sins."

Exegetical Notes

- Paul explains Israel's partial rejection of Christ is temporary and partial, allowing gentiles to be grafted into God's people during the church age.
- The "fullness of the gentiles" marks the completion of the church age and sets the stage for Israel's corporate salvation.
- The promise that "all Israel will be saved" anticipates a future turning of Israel to Christ.
- The church age is a "parenthesis" in God's plan, with irrevocable promises still held for Israel (see Rom 11:29).
- This view harmonizes with the hope of Israel's ultimate restoration and salvation at the end of the age.

5. Daniel 9:24-27—The Prophecy of the Seventy Weeks

Passage (ESV)

24 Seventy weeks are decreed about your people and your holy city, to finish the transgression, to put an end to sin, to atone for iniquity, to bring in everlasting righteousness, to seal both vision and prophet, and to anoint a most holy place.

25 Know therefore and understand that from the going out of the word to restore and build Jerusalem to the coming of an anointed one, a prince, there shall be

seven weeks. Then for sixty-two weeks it shall be built again with squares and moat, but in a troubled time.

26 And after the sixty-two weeks, an anointed one shall be cut off and shall have nothing. And the people of the prince who is to come shall destroy the city and the sanctuary. Its end shall come with a flood, and to the end there shall be war. Desolations are decreed.

27 And he shall make a strong covenant with many for one week, and for half of the week he shall put an end to sacrifice and offering. And on a wing of the temple shall be an abomination that makes desolate, until the decreed end is poured out on the desolator.

Exegetical Notes

- The prophecy sets a divinely appointed timetable for Israel and Jerusalem, consisting of seventy "weeks" (typically interpreted as sets of seven years) in which God's redemptive plan unfolds.

- The first sixty-nine weeks culminate in the coming and death of the Messiah, Jesus Christ, fulfilling messianic expectations.

- The final "week" is seen as a future seven-year tribulation, involving the antichrist's covenant, cessation of temple sacrifices, and the "abomination of desolation."

- This final period corresponds with the "little while" in Rev 20, marking intense tribulation before Christ's return.

- The prophecy supports a literal rebuilding of Jerusalem and the temple, reinforcing the dispensational amillennial view that the church age is intercalated within God's plan for Israel.

- The antichrist's covenant and subsequent breaking serve as a central element of end-times deception and judgment.

Exegesis of Key Texts from the Dispensational Amillennial Perspective

6. Isaiah 65:17-25—The Glorious New Creation

Passage (ESV)

> 17 For behold, I create new heavens and a new earth, and the former things shall not be remembered or come into mind. 18 But be glad and rejoice forever in that which I create; for behold, I create Jerusalem to be a joy, and her people to be a gladness. 19 I will rejoice in Jerusalem and be glad in my people; no more shall be heard in it the sound of weeping and the cry of distress. 20 No more shall there be in it an infant who lives but a few days, or an old man who does not fill out his days, for the young man shall die a hundred years old, 21 They shall build houses and inhabit them; they shall plant vineyards and eat their fruit. They shall not build and another inhabit; 22 they shall not plant and another eat; for like the days of a tree shall the days of my people be, and my chosen shall long enjoy the work of their hands. 23 They shall not labor in vain or bear children for calamity, for they shall be the offspring of the blessed of the LORD, and their descendants with them. 24 Before they call I will answer; while they are yet speaking, I will hear. 25 The wolf and the lamb shall graze together; the lion shall eat straw like the ox, and dust shall be the serpent's food; they shall not hurt or destroy in all my holy mountain, says the LORD.

Exegetical Notes

a. Creation of New Heavens and New Earth (v. 17)

- The verb *create* (אָרָב, *bara*) emphasizes *divine initiative*—God alone brings about a reality wholly renewed.
- The phrase "former things shall not be remembered" indicates the *finality of redemption* and the obliteration of sin and sorrow.

Millennium in the Middle

- This is not a temporary, earthly restoration; it parallels Rev 21:1–5, where John sees the *new Jerusalem descending from heaven*, signaling ultimate consummation.

b. Joyful Restoration and Covenant Fulfillment (vv. 18–19)

- Jerusalem becomes a source of joy, and its people experience gladness.
- The language of building houses, planting vineyards, and long enjoyment (vv. 21–22) *echoes Old Testament covenant promises* (Lev 26:11–12; Deut 30:9) but transposes them into *an eternal, perfected context*.
- In dispensational-amillennial terms, this is *the fulfillment of God's promises to Israel and the redeemed*, but in a consummated, eternal perspective rather than a temporal thousand-year kingdom.

c. Already, but Not Yet (v. 20)

- The "hundred years" is not literal but symbolizes *fullness of life and blessing* under God's covenant.
- In a dispensational framework, this "full life" is tied to *God's unfolding plan in history*, showing continuity between the present church age and the final consummation.
- Christ's reign is *present now* (amillennial aspect) but also tied to historical dispensations.
- Believers experience the spiritual blessings of God's kingdom now (peace, growth, protection), even as the world still struggles under sin and death
- "The sinner . . . shall be accursed" demonstrates *God's moral order across dispensations.*
- Sin is restrained (Satan's binding) during the present church age, but full judgment awaits Christ's return.

Exegesis of Key Texts from the Dispensational Amillennial Perspective

- This aligns with dispensationalism in recognizing *different phases of God's redemptive plan*, where the present age is preparatory to the final consummation.

d. Divine Response and Peace (vv. 23–25)

- God promises immediate and intimate hearing: "Before they call I will answer" (v. 24).
- Peace is described universally: predators and prey coexist; the serpent is subdued (v. 25).
- Such imagery is *symbolic of the removal of sin, death, and conflict*—not merely the social or political restoration of Israel on earth.
- This aligns with amillennial understanding that the *"holy mountain"* refers to God's eternal dominion, fulfilled in the final state.

Closing Remarks

This exegesis reflects how the dispensational amillennial perspective interprets key prophetic and eschatological passages, emphasizing both spiritual realities present in the church age and the literal future fulfillment of God's promises to Israel. It underscores the harmony between biblical prophecy and the hope of Christ's return, encouraging careful, Scripture-centered interpretation that honors the complexity and unity of God's redemptive plan.

Bibliography

Augustine. *The City of God*. Translated by Henry Bettenson. London: Penguin, 1972.

Baucham, Voddie. "When Is the Millennium?" Grace Family Baptist Church, Dec. 22, 2013. https://www.sermonaudio.com/sermons/1230131011156.

Borlaug, Norman E. "Nobel Prize Lecture: The Green Revolution, Peace, and Humanity." Norwegian Nobel Institute, Dec. 11, 1970. https://www.nobelprize.org/prizes/peace/1970/borlaug/lecture/.

Calvin, John. *Institutes of the Christian Religion*. Edited by John T. McNeill. Translated by Ford Lewis Battles. Philadelphia: Westminster, 1960.

Christian Reformed Church. *The Belgic Confession of Faith*. Grand Rapids: Faith Alive Christian Resources, 2011. https://www.crcna.org/welcome/beliefs/confessions/belgic-confession.

———. *Heidelberg Catechism*. Grand Rapids: Faith Alive Christian Resources, 2011. https://www.crcna.org/welcome/beliefs/confessions/heidelberg-catechism.

Eze, Jerry Uchechukwu. "Jesus Reigns . . . I haven't recovered yet. People blocked streets to find a place to stand. People hung on trees and roofs of houses just to witness the Power of Jesus." Facebook reel, Apr. 5, 2025. https://www.facebook.com/jerryuchechukwu.ezeii/posts/zambiazambiazambiajesus-reignsi-havent-recovered-yet-people-blocked-streets-to-f/1239076307582414/.

Horton, Michael S. *Introducing Covenant Theology*. Grand Rapids: Baker, 2006.

Luther, Martin. *Commentary on Galatians*. Translated by Theodore Graebner. Grand Rapids: Zondervan, 1949.

———. *Selections from the Table Talk of Martin Luther*. Edited by Henry Bell. eBook ed. Aug. 24, 2014. https://www.gutenberg.org/files/9841/9841-h/9841-h.htm.

Bibliography

Piper, John. "An Evening of Eschatology: Premillennialism, Amillennialism, Postmillennialism." Desiring God, Sept. 27, 2009. https://www.desiringgod.org/interviews/an-evening-of-eschatology.

———. "How Soon Is Christ's Return?" Desiring God, Feb. 22, 2017. https://www.desiringgod.org/interviews/how-soon-is-christs-return.

Riddlebarger, Kim. *A Case for Amillennialism: Understanding the End Times*. Grand Rapids: Baker, 2003.

Sproul, R. C. *The Last Days According to Jesus*. Grand Rapids: Baker, 1998.

Storms, Sam. *Kingdom Come: The Amillennial Alternative*. Fearn, UK: Christian Focus, 2013.

Tertullian. *Apologeticus*. Translated by S. Thelwall. In *Ante-Nicene Fathers*, edited by Alexander Roberts and James Donaldson, 3. Buffalo: Christian Literature, 1885. https://www.newadvent.org/fathers/0301.htm.

Westminster Assembly. *The Westminster Confession of Faith and Catechisms*. Lawrenceville, GA: Christian Education & Publications, 2007. https://www.pcaac.org/resources/wcf/.

Wycliffe Global Alliance. "2024 Global Scripture Access." https://wycliffe.net/global-scripture-access/.

www.ingramcontent.com/pod-product-compliance
Lightning Source LLC
Chambersburg PA
CBHW051104160426
43193CB00010B/1314